MINI

MUNICH & BAVARIA

How to download your Free eBook

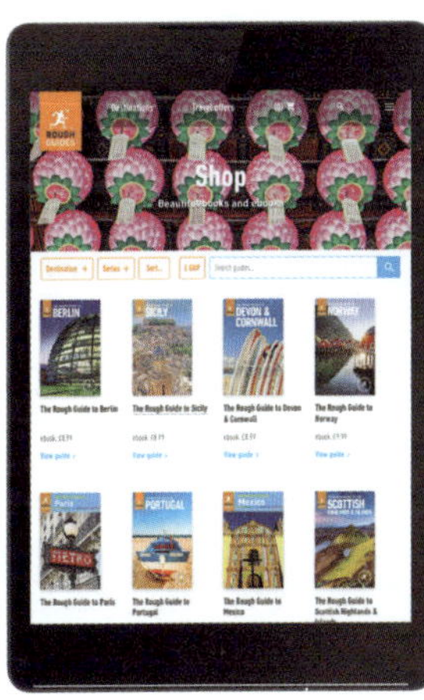

1. Visit **www.roughguides.com/free-ebook** or scan the **QR code** opposite
2. Enter the code **munich501**
3. Follow the simple step-by-step instructions

For troubleshooting contact: mail@roughguides.com

Contents

Introduction

With its relaxed, almost Mediterranean ambience, Munich is one of Europe's most engaging cities. The Bavarian capital is packed with fascinating history, world-class culture and traditional food, with the outdoor playground of the Alps just a short hop away.

The city's genius has always been its ability to combine the Germanic talent for getting things done with a specifically Bavarian need to do so in an agreeable way. Business lunches linger a little longer here, office hours tend to be shorter. Yet no one who has witnessed the city's impressive affluence, its dynamic car industry and its super-efficient public-transport system would suggest that this refreshingly relaxed attitude was unproductive.

Playing volleyball in Englischer Garten

Munich and Bavaria are Germany's most popular tourist destinations. According to opinion polls, Munich is also the city that Germans would most like to call home. It is not just the elegance and prosperity of the place that make it such a magnet, but the lively way of life that is best savoured in one of its many beer gardens, beer halls or just out and about on the town, particularly during the long, hot summers. As the capital of the Catholic and conservative Free State of Bavaria, Munich epitomises the independent

WHAT'S NEW

While several of Munich's large museums and institutions are currently undergoing multiyear renovation projects, a cluster of interesting new developments have sprung up on the fringes of the city centre. In Schwabing, the lively Elisabethmarkt (www.elisabethmarkt.de) has reopened with a brand-new set of market stalls selling delicious regional food and drinks, many of them organic. Near Leonrodplatz, the Kreativquartier is an emerging district studded with cultural institutes, restaurants and social projects. South of the centre in Isarvorstadt, the Schlachthofviertel former slaughterhouse area is gradually being transformed into a thriving neighbourhood of local residences, a park, street art and culture, all anchored around the new Volkstheater (www.muenchner-volkstheater.de). Finally, the venerable Gasteig cultural centre (www.gasteig.de) has moved south of the city centre, rebranding itself as Gasteig HP8, a shiny venue with impressive concert and event halls. It will serve as the temporary home for arts events and exhibitions while renovations are ongoing at the original (see page 74).

Bavarian spirit, but it is also a highly cosmopolitan city, where people from all over the world feel at home.

Of course, Munich also plays host to the iconic Oktoberfest, usually the single event that springs to mind when anyone mentions the city's name. Indeed, with 3.6 million visitors guzzling seven million litres of beer, it is a blockbuster annual event. It is also the most extravagant expression of that untranslatable feeling of warm fellowship known in German as *Gemütlichkeit.*

Cultural centre

But it would be wrong to think of life in Munich merely as one long Oktoberfest. As a result of the postwar division of Berlin, Munich became the undisputed cultural capital of the Federal Republic of Germany – no mean achievement in the face of competition from

Cycling past the Glyptothek

NOTES

Munich is the capital of Bavaria and of the administrative district of Upper Bavaria. It is draped across a plain to the north of the Alpine foothills, about 530m (1700ft) above sea level. The population of the city, which spreads across 310 sq km (120 sq miles), is just over 1.5 million, making the Bavarian metropolis the third-largest city in Germany, trailing only Berlin and Hamburg.

Hamburg and Cologne. The opera house and concert halls give the town some serious musical chops, with a fine programme of performances of works by Richard Strauss, Mozart and Wagner. Wagner's patron was King Ludwig II of Bavaria, the mastermind behind the fairy-tale Neuschwanstein Castle in the Alpine foothills, but it was his grandfather, Ludwig I, who established

SUSTAINABLE TRAVEL

It's easy to travel sustainably in Germany. Travelling by train instead of flying is the most significant way to reduce your impact on the planet; the trip from London takes 8hr 30min (see www.seat61.com for booking options). On arrival, excellent and affordable public transport means you won't need a car to explore Munich and the surroundings. The €58 Deutschland-Ticket (www.germanytransitpass.com), valid for all local and regional public transport throughout Germany for a calendar month, can be great value if you're planning on venturing further afield. Nextbike (www.nextbike.de) offers bikes for rent across Munich. If you'd like to invest time in a social project, Vostel (www.vostel.de) lists various volunteering options.

the city's cultural credentials by assembling vast art collections and building huge edifices in which to store them.

That legacy lives on in Munich, and the city is endowed with world-famous collections, from the Old Masters of the Alte Pinakothek to the avant-garde movements represented in the Pinakothek der Moderne and Museum Brandhorst. Painters have long appreciated the favourable artistic climate of the city, particularly in the bohemian district of Schwabing, which exploded onto the international scene in the early twentieth century as a centre for the Blaue Reiter school, whose ranks included Wassily Kandinsky, Paul Klee and Franz Marc.

Munich has become a hub for industry and publishing, and also for the much-admired New German Cinema and its world-famous directors, Volker Schloendorff, Werner Herzog and Edgar Reitz. But there is a darker side to the city, including Adolf Hitler's early association with Munich and the formation here of the Nazi Party. After the harrowing period of 1918 to 1945, Munich's people seem happy to have relinquished the political limelight to Bonn and Berlin.

Restored heritage

Munich has tried, however, to retain its historical identity. After the destruction of World War II, many German cities decided to break with the past and rebuild in a completely modern style. But the authorities in the Bavarian capital chose to painstakingly restore and reconstruct its great churches and palaces. While contemporary office blocks cluster along the city's periphery, the heart of the historic core has successfully recaptured its rich architectural heritage and charm. There are still reminders of the ravages of war, and monuments such as the Siegestor (Victory Gate, in Ludwigstrasse) have been left in their bomb-scarred condition as a haunting reminder of more troubled days.

Glockenspiel, Neues Rathaus

WHEN TO GO

Germany straddles the maritime climates of the Western European seaboard and the more extreme conditions found further east. June, July and August are the warmest and busiest months in Munich, though midsummer is also when the city receives its highest rainfall, so showers are highly likely. For more predictable weather, with plenty of sunshine and comfortable temperatures, the shoulder seasons of late spring and early autumn – May, September and early October – are well worth considering. Plus, the Germans don't call the harvest season "goldener Oktober" for nothing – it's a beautiful time to visit. The ski season in the Alps runs between Christmas and the end of March.

The inner city is a pedestrian's delight, thanks to a clever road system that keeps the majority of traffic circling the centre rather than crossing through it (except by means of underpasses). It also has an excellent public transport system. Beyond the centre the broad, tree-lined avenues and boulevards planned by Bavaria's last kings open up the town and add an elegant touch to the cityscape.

Open spaces

The Englischer Garten, set between several tributaries of the River Isar, is a real jewel among Europe's great parks. The swiftly flowing waters nod to the proximity of the Alps, which conceals the source of the river. On a clear day, the mountains appear to lie just south of the city. When the peaks loom on the city's doorstep, locals are reminded of the countryside from which many of them, or their parents, originated. Every weekend a mass exodus to the surrounding villages and lakes takes place. In the winter many head further south into the wilderness for skiing, an integral part of Bavarian life. Although Munich is undoubtedly a metropolis, the city also retains a resolutely rural atmosphere, never losing sight of its roots in the Bavarian hinterland.

10 Things not to miss

7

8

9

10

1 **PINAKOTHEK DER MODERNE**
The largest museum of art and design in Europe. See page 67.

2 **ENGLISCHER GARTEN**
Featuring the Chinese Tower and its beer garden. See page 71.

3 **MARIENPLATZ**
Munich's main square with the Column of the Virgin Mary at its centre. See page 39.

4 **ALTER PETER**
Munich's oldest church provides fine views of the city and the Alps. See page 43.

5 **DEUTSCHES MUSEUM**
World-class museum of science and technology. See page 76.

6 **ASAMKIRCHE**
A theatrical masterpiece of sculpture, decoration and light, created by the Asam brothers. See page 50.

7 **KÖNIGSSEE**
Southern Germany's most attractive and pristine body of water cradled by the High Alps. See page 90.

8 **ALTE PINAKOTHEK**
One of the world's top art galleries. See page 65.

9 **RESIDENZ**
The former royal palace, with seven courtyards and the magnificent Renaissance hall, the Antiquarium. See page 53.

10 **NEUSCHWANSTEIN CASTLE**
Ludwig II's extraordinary romanticised version of the medieval world. See page 86.

A perfect day in Munich

9AM

Breakfast. A traditional breakfast of sausage with sweet mustard and soft pretzel is the way to start the Munich day; head for *Wildmosers* (Marienplatz 22), which specialises in local speciality, the humble Weisswurst.

10AM

The Residenz. Kick off your day of Munich sightseeing at the Residenz, right in the city centre. You'll need at least two hours to cover the trio of attractions here – the Residenzmuseum, the Schatzkammer and the Cuvilliés-Theater.

12.30PM

Chic shopping. Time to hit the smart boutiques and designer shops at Maximilianstrasse. Window shop along Residenzstrasse and Theatinerstrasse, by which time you'll have worked up a hearty appetite.

1.30PM

Lunch. Stave off hunger pangs with some traditional Bavarian fare at *Weisses Bräuhaus* (see page 124) or lighter, more innovative vegetarian dishes at *Prince Myshkin* (see page 123).

2.30PM

Modern art. After lunch, walk to the Museum Quarter for a hefty dose of culture. You'll only have time to view a couple of the many venues here, so choose carefully beforehand. Fans of contemporary art and design should beeline for the multicoloured Museum Brandhorst and view Andy Warhol's paintings. Refuel in the old-style museum café at the nearby Alte Pinakothek.

4.30PM

Beer gardens. Time for a break, so take a short walk from the art action to the Englischer Garten for a tranquil amble and a laze with the locals on the grass, perhaps stopping off at the *Chinesischer Turm* (see page 126) for a coffee or something stronger. Afterwards, leave the park to the south to see the river surfers riding the wave of the Eisbach stream.

6PM

Bavarian dinner. The perfect place to eat and drink your fill is one of the city's inimitable beer halls. For the full-on tourist experience you could plump for the *Hofbräuhaus* (see page 122); for something a bit more authentic try the *Augustiner Bräustuben* (see page 124) near Hackerbrücke S-Bahn station (or three stops from the Hauptbahnhof on trams 18 and 19).

8.30PM

A slice of nightlife. Round off the day with a chilled evening at one of the city's excellent jazz joints. *Unterfahrt im Einstein* and *Mister B's* (see page 103) are the foot-tapping venues of choice. If jazz is not to your taste, then a more eclectic scene can be found in the bars of the Gärtnerplatzviertel and around Münchner Freiheit square in Schwabing.

Budget Munich

7AM

Endorphins and eggs. Kickstart the day with a free summertime session of yoga, qigong or pilates in one of Munich's urban parks (www.muenchen.de). Refuel with food to go from one of Munich's affordable cafés and bakeries, or pick up fresh, local produce in the likes of Viktualienmarkt or the Elisabethmarkt.

10AM

Guided walk. Embark on a free city tour to see Munich through a local lens; try Walkative (https://freewalkingtour.com) or Heart of Munich (https://heartofmunich.com). Bring a reusable bottle to fill with 'M-Wasser', free drinking water sourced from natural springs in the Alpine foothills.

NOON

Birthday perks. If your visit happens to fall on your birthday, take advantage of complimentary admission to the FC Bayern Museum (https://fcbayern.com/museum) or the Olympiaturm tower.

1PM

Lunch. Hotfoot it to one of the university *Menses* (cafeterias), which are open to all and serve decent meals at low prices; the *Mensa Arcisstraße* (Arcisstraße 17) is a central option.

2PM

Culture. If you're under 18, entry to many museums is free. Failing that, plump for a Sunday to pay €1 admission at many venues. Browse Egyptian art treasures at the Pinakotheken; ancient Greek sculpture at Glyptothek (see page 62); or ethnological displays at Fünf Kontinente (see page 75).

4PM

Art riches. Several galleries in Munich are always free. Perhaps check out contemporary art in the Rathausgalerie (www.rathausgalerie-muenchen.de) or celebrate street art in the AMUSEUM of Contemporary Art (https://visit-amuseum.com).

5PM

Wild swim. Wash off the day's exertions with a refreshing dip in the icy waters of the River Isar – if you dare.

6PM

Dinner. For dinner, head to one of the city's kebab, falafel or burger joints for a cheap, filling meal. Alternatively, grab a seat and a beer in one of the city's famous *Biergartens*, but bring your own food to keep costs down.

7PM

Concerts. When there's a concert on at the Olympiastadion, claim a patch of grass in the adjacent Olympiaberg and listen along for free. Alternatively, emerging local and international bands and artists are staged at the Muffathalle's free Munich Rocks gigs, and also during the Olympiaparks Theatron Musiksommer.

Alpine adventure

7.30AM

Serene train journey. To make the most of a day in Germany's most stunning alpine scenery, catch an early train to Garmisch-Partenkirchen, a scenic 1hr 30min journey offering glimpses of glassy Lake Starnberg and the formidable High Alps. The bakeries at Munich's railway station can provide a delicious breakfast spread to enjoy on board.

9.30AM

Reaching new heights. From Garmisch-Partenkirchen, walk over to the Zugspitzbahn station, buy a ticket for a return trip (or a single if you want to hike in one direction) and hop on the hourly Zugspitzplatt cog railway train that slowly grinds its way up the valley.

9.45AM

Cable car, optional. You have the option to disembark at Eibsee station and take the cable car (included in train ticket) to the 2962m (2468ft) summit of Zugspitze, Germany's highest peak. Expect excellent views as you scale the 3.2km (2 mile) journey on the world's longest free-hanging cable, suspended from a 127m (416ft) steel pylon – the tallest of its kind, no less. If you decide to stay on the train, you'll burrow through the mountain via a long tunnel.

10AM

Fine views. At the lofty summit of Zugspitze, you can take in panoramic vistas, have lunch with a view, browse an exhibition on the history of tourism in this corner of the Alps, and even wander across the border to the Austrian mountain station. Beautiful alpine walks and hikes start at Zugspitzplatt station, and in winter there's tobogganing.

NOON

Lake walks. Take the cable car or cog railway back down, then spend a few hours hiking around the crystal-clear Eibsee alpine lake, with great views of Zugspitze.

2PM

Lüftlmalerei galore. Return to Garmisch-Partenkirchen and walk to Ludwigstrasse in the town centre, where nearly every building facade is splashed with Lüftlmalerei paintings. Alternatively, continue by regional train to Mittenwald, a charming small town cradled in the belly of a wide valley; here, you can also admire Lüftlmalerei as well as visit the quirky Geigenbaumuseum (Violin Museum; www.geigenbaumuseum-mittenwald.de).

5.30PM

Return journey. It's time to head back to Munich. Either, take the train as before or you could hop on bus 9608 from Mittenwald, which skirts the sublime shores of Walchensee lake to Kochel station, from where there are hourly trains on to Munich.

History

Munich was a relatively late arrival on the Bavarian scene. During the Middle Ages, at a time when Nuremberg, Augsburg, Landshut and Regensburg were already thriving cities, the present-day state capital was no more than a small settlement housing a community of Benedictine monks from Tegernsee. The site was known in the eighth century quite simply as *Ze den Munichen*, a dialect form of *zu den Mönchen* ('the monks' place'). Accordingly, Munich's coat of arms today bears the image of a child in a monk's habit, the Münchner Kindl.

In 1158, the settlement on the River Isar caught the eye of Heinrich der Löwe (Henry the Lion), the Duke of Saxony and Bavaria, who was cousin of the German Emperor Frederick Barbarossa. He was searching for a place to set up a toll station for the passage of salt, a lucrative product from nearby Salzburg. Until then, tolls had been collected by the powerful bishop of Freising at Oberföhring Bridge, just to the north. Duke Heinrich burned this bridge down and built a new one, together with a market, customs house and mint.

Bishop Otto of Freising, an uncle of Frederick Barbarossa, protested to the emperor, who decided to leave Munich in Heinrich's hands, but to grant one-third of the toll revenues to the diocese of Freising – dues that were paid until 1852. The day of the emperor's decision, 14 June 1158, is recognised as the date of Munich's foundation.

Munich grew into a prosperous town off the back of the lucrative salt trade. In 1180, after Heinrich refused military aid for the emperor's foreign wars, Frederick Barbarossa threatened to raze Munich to the ground. However, Bishop Otto pleaded the city's case, as he was making a great deal of money from his share of the salt duty. Munich was saved, but the city was handed over to the Wittelsbach family, who ruled Bavaria for the next seven centuries.

The Wittelsbachs take over

The coronation of Ludwig of Bavaria, 1328

By the end of the thirteenth century, Munich was the largest town in the Wittelsbach dominions. However, the wealthy Munich burghers grew discontented and began to press Duke Ludwig the Stern (1229–94) for a larger piece of the pie. In defence, the duke built himself a fortress, the Alter Hof, parts of which still stand near Marienplatz. Munich stepped onto the international political stage in 1328, when Duke Ludwig IV (1294–1347) was made Holy Roman Emperor. With his court firmly established in Munich, he enlisted scholars from all over Europe as his advisors. Perhaps the most notable of these were Marsiglio of Padua and the English Franciscan friar William of Occam, both philosophers who defended secular power against that of the Pope and thus made themselves useful allies for Ludwig.

Troubled times

The Black Death wreaked devastation in 1348. Social unrest and abrupt economic decline ensued. In a wildly irrational reaction to the catastrophe, citizens embarked on a violent rampage, massacring Jews for alleged ritual murder.

High taxes triggered the burghers to revolt against the patricians. In 1385, the people beheaded a cloth merchant, Hans Impler, on the Schrannenplatz (now Marienplatz); the patricians and their princes demanded financial compensation; and the situation deteriorated into open rebellion from 1397 to 1403.

NOTES

Regarded as one of the major figures of medieval thought, William of Occam is best known for 'Occam's razor', in which he states, roughly, that if you've found a simple explanation for a problem, don't look for a complicated one. Bavarians like that kind of thinking.

Bringing in heavy military reinforcements, the Wittelsbachs regained the upper hand without being forced to make the far-reaching civic concessions won by the guilds in other German cities. To secure their position during these troubled times, the Wittelsbachs built a sturdy fortress, the Residenz, on what was then the northern edge of town.

Reform and counter-reform

Dissent eased in the fifteenth century, and the salt, wine and cloth trade boomed. The town also established itself as a transit point for spices and gold. The great Frauenkirche and the Gothic civic citadel of the Altes Rathaus, were built during this period of renewed prosperity.

By the mid-sixteenth century, architectural rivalry was simmering between the burghers – who favoured the German Gothic style for their homes – and the Bavarian nobles, who were drawn to the Renaissance flourishes of Southern Europe. The appearance of Munich in the 1500s is immortalised in Jakob Sandtner's city model, now on display in the Bavarian National Museum. However, most of the original buildings were later replaced by the Baroque and Rococo palaces of the seventeenth and eighteenth centuries and the neo-Gothic and Neoclassical buildings of the Industrial Revolution.

The Bavarian aristocracy's preference for foreign styles was in many ways a reaction to the subversive implications of German nationalism, which had grown out of the Reformation. In 1510, when Martin Luther passed through Munich on his way to Rome, his still relatively orthodox preaching was met with sympathy. But some ten years later, Luther's revolutionary position aroused the anger of the traditionally conservative Bavarians, and Duke Wilhelm IV introduced the severe measures advocated by the Jesuits. Rebellious monks and priests were arrested and executed.

The religious conflict concealed a competition for political and economic power. The city's bourgeoisie had seen in the Reformation an opportunity to push for the social reforms that the aristocracy had adamantly resisted. In the struggles that followed, the burghers were forced to relinquish the salt monopoly to the administration of the state.

With a certain vindictiveness, the nobles flaunted their political triumph with sumptuous festivities in court, such as those arranged to pay homage to Emperor Charles V and his Spanish retinue during their visit in 1530. The climax of such pomp and circumstance was the three-week-long wedding celebration of Duke Wilhelm V and his bride, Renata of Lorraine, in 1568.

The towers of the Frauenkirche

Good money after bad

Such extravagant expenditure meant that the state coffers were empty by the

The Antiquarium in the Residenz, built around 1570

time Maximilian I (1573–1651) rose to the throne. Despite this lack of funds, Maximilian (who was made Prince Elector in 1623) managed to build up a magnificent collection of artworks. However painful this may have been for his tax-crippled subjects, today's citizens can be thankful to him for having laid the foundations of the Alte Pinakothek.

It was also Maximilian who ordered the splendid decorations that embellish the Residenz. Gustavus Adolphus of Sweden, who invaded Munich in 1632 during the cruel Thirty Years' War, was so impressed with the Residenz that he voiced a wish to wheel the whole thing back to Stockholm. Instead, he settled for 42 Munich citizens, who were taken hostage against payment by Bavaria of 300,000 Thaler in war reparations. All but six of them returned three years later.

The Thirty Years' War (1618–48) caused less damage in Munich, however, than in many other German towns. Nonetheless, starvation and disease wrought more havoc than the cannon. In 1634 the Black Death struck, killing seven thousand inhabitants – a third of the city's population. In 1638, Maximilian set up the Mariensäule (Column of the Virgin Mary) as thanks for the city's deliverance.

Munich's Prince Electors frequently involved the city in costly foreign adventures, thus rubbing salt into the wounds of civic poverty. In 1683, Maximilian II Emanuel decided to help the Austrians beat off the Turks besieging Vienna. He promptly set out for Belgrade, returning with 296 Turks who were indentured as sedan-chair bearers and roadbuilders. The Turkish Wars are commemorated in huge paintings on display in Schleissheim Castle. The city was saddled with an immense debt because of the war.

The Theatinerkirche, built between 1663 and 1690, a Munich landmark

During the War of the Spanish Succession (1701–14), Maximilian II Emanuel fought, along with the French, on the losing side and Munich had to bear the unfortunate burden of Austrian occupation from 1704 to 1714. When the farmers rebelled in 1705, the ringleaders were arrested and hanged, drawn and quartered on Marienplatz.

After the war, the Bavarian aristocracy was not especially

sympathetic to the tribulations of the citizenry. Palaces sprung up along the city streets, including the Preysing Palais, the Archbishop's Palais and the Törring-Jettenbach Palais.

Peace in an English garden

The people of Munich grew ever more xenophobic after Hungarian hussars seized the city in 1742. They were dispatched by Empress Maria Theresa in retaliation for the Bavarian Prince Elector's opposition to Austro-Hungarian involvement in Germany.

Amid this simmering hostility, Maximilian III Joseph (1727–77) could not have been surprised when the Munich bourgeoisie resisted his efforts to establish a court monopoly on the manufacture of goods. Royal manufacturers were plunged into bankruptcy, with the exception of Nymphenburg porcelain (still a thriving concern). A brighter note was struck with the building of the delightful Cuvilliés-Theater and the performance here by one Wolfgang Amadeus Mozart of his operas *Idomeneo* (premiered in 1781), *The Abduction from the Seraglio*, *The Marriage of Figaro* and *The Magic Flute*.

When Maximilian III Joseph, the last of the true Wittelsbach line, died in 1777, the succession fell to Karl Theodor, a member of the Mannheim branch of the family. He wasn't keen, however, to leave his home: he didn't like Munich and Munich didn't like him. The people were starving. Instead of bread, Karl Theodor sent in soldiers to suppress the angry populace.

It was Benjamin Thompson, an American, who suggested a solution to Karl Theodor's predicament. With the prince's blessing, Count Rumford (as he was subsequently known) provided schools and work to keep the unruly soldiers off the streets. He set up workshops and soup kitchens for the poor. In 1789, Rumford requisitioned a marshy wilderness on the outskirts of town and ordered the soldiers to drain it for development as gardens and a gigantic public park – today's Englischer Garten.

Hopes and dreams

While Munich was gardening, Europe was in revolutionary uproar and the city could not remain immune to these events for long. In 1800 it was occupied by the French troops of General Jean Victor Moreau, who established his headquarters in Nymphenburg Palace.

Napoleon himself arrived in 1805 for the wedding of his wife Josephine's son, Eugène de Beauharnais, to Princess Augusta. The emperor was on his way to Austerlitz (in today's Czech Republic), where he was to fight the Russians and Austrians. Napoleon elevated Maximilian IV Joseph from Prince Elector to King of Bavaria, and in exchange took a vast contingent of Bavarians on his Russian campaign of 1812. Under pressure from the French, Maximilian

'View of Munich' by Bernardo Bellotto (c. 1761)

emancipated the Protestants of Munich, improved conditions for Jewish people and introduced a more moderate constitution.

Despite the troubles of war and revolution, Munich managed to celebrate once again. Heeding the new spirit of the times, the royal court chose not to exclude the populace from the celebrations in honour of the marriage of Maximilian's son, Ludwig, to Theresa of Saxony. On 17 October 1810, horseraces were organised, with great success. These morphed into an annual event, which became known as Oktoberfest.

Munich itself was gradually mushrooming north and west into Maxvorstadt, a district that connects the city centre to Schwabing. The Graeco-Roman architecture of the Nationaltheater brought to the city the first signs of the Classical spirit that was to become the obsession of Ludwig I.

Ludwig II

Born in Strasbourg, Ludwig (1786–1868) was determined to break the French stranglehold on German culture and to position Munich as the leader of a new nationalist movement. During the Napoleonic occupation, the civic symbol of the Münchner Kindl had been replaced with an imperial lion; Ludwig quickly restored the little monk.

Familiar with the architecture of Greece and Rome, Ludwig was determined to

HER NAME WAS LOLA

A prodigious worker, rising before dawn each day to go to his office in the Residenz, Ludwig I gained some diversion from his sober duties by commissioning a series of portraits of the most beautiful young women of Munich. The collection hangs in the Schönheitsgalerie (Gallery of Beautiful Women) at the Nymphenburg Palace. Included is his mistress, a dancer known as Lola Montez, with whom he fell in love when he was 60 and she 28. She was Ludwig's ruin. He made her the Countess von Landsfeld, to the horror both of his conservative ministers and the radical university students.

In 1848, as revolution swept Europe, the students and angry citizens of Munich forced Ludwig to deport Lola, and he abdicated in disgust. The story of Lola's fascinatingly eventful life is told in the book *Lola Montez: A Life* by Bruce Seymour.

turn Munich into an 'Athens-on-the-Isar'. His first step was to move Bavaria's university from Landshut to Munich, where it was established along Ludwigstrasse.

Königsplatz, with its Greek Revival architecture, was the most complete realisation of Ludwig's Classical aspirations. Typically, Ludwig himself laid the foundation stone for the Alte Pinakothek (the gallery designed to house the royal art collections) on 7 April 1826, the anniversary of the painter Raphael's birth. Ludwig's successor, Maximilian II (1811– 64), boosted Munich's cultural reputation thanks to his intimacy with illustrious thinkers such as the historian Leopold von Ranke, the philosopher Friedrich von Schelling and the chemist Justus von Liebig.

End of a dream

The last great king of Bavaria was the romantic king Ludwig II (1845–86), famous for his collaboration with Richard Wagner. Under Ludwig's patronage, the composer staged in Munich the

'Der Blaue Reiter' by Wassily Kandinsky

premières of his operas *Tristan und Isolde*, *Die Meistersinger von Nürnberg*, *Das Rheingold* and *Die Walküre*.

In the mundane world of nineteenth-century industrial expansion, Ludwig dreamt of making Munich the music capital of the world. He wanted to build a gigantic theatre for his idol Wagner, a place where the composer could develop his concept of *gesamtkunstwerk* – a synthesis of music, lyrics and theatre. State finances forced him to relinquish the project to Bayreuth.

Ludwig acted out his fantasies in the eccentric palaces he built outside Munich – a medieval castle at Neuschwanstein, a beautiful French château at Linderhof and a fanciful version of Versailles' Grand Trianon at Herrenchiemsee (more were planned). Ironically, it was at the sixteenth-century castle, Schloss Berg by Lake Starnberg, that Ludwig's life came to a mysterious end. By

1886, his unorthodox behaviour had persuaded the Bavarian government that he was mentally unstable, and a special commission 'confirmed' this. The director of a mental health institution accompanied him to Schloss Berg but the two were later found drowned. Was it murder or suicide? The speculation continues to this day.

Uncle Luitpold took over as regent (in place of Ludwig's brother, King Otto). He presided over the grand fin de siècle artistic movement of the *Jugendstil*. This was followed a generation later by the *Blaue Reiter* (Blue Rider) school, which included Wassily Kandinsky, Paul Klee, Franz Marc and Gabriele Münter. Thomas Mann, Rainer Maria Rilke, Stefan George and other writers moved to Schwabing. The artistic ferment also attracted a painter from Vienna, a young man named Adolf Hitler.

The Wittelsbach dynasty, along with others in Vienna and Berlin, ended in the disaster of World War I. Bavarians resented having been dragged into the European conflict by what they felt was Prussian belligerence, and a new social democratic movement gained support. In November 1918, Kurt Eisner led a march of workers and peasants from the Theresienwiese. En route, disaffected soldiers took control of their barracks and hoisted the red flag of revolution. The Bavarian Socialist Republic was declared in the Mathäser Bräuhaus. The people invaded the Residenz and Ludwig III, the last Wittelsbach king, fled in a car from the palace.

But the newly born republic of workers, peasants and soldiers, modelled on the Soviets created under the Russian revolution, was subject to violent attack from the conservative press and from private armies of troops (*freikorps*). Playing on Bavarian xenophobia, the right-wing attacked Eisner as a Berliner and as a Jew. Just three months after the November revolution, Eisner was dead, shot down by a young aristocrat hoping to curry favour with an extreme right-wing club.

A group of 'coffee-house anarchists' led by the writers Ernst Toller and Erich Mühsam took over briefly, but they were soon

BEER, BLUFF AND BULLETS

The Beer Hall Putsch, which launched Hitler's national career, was staged in the now-defunct Bürgerbräukeller. It gave a foretaste of the crazy melodrama, bluff and shameless gall he was later to exhibit on the world scene.

With the Bavarian minister Gustav von Kahr about to speak, Hitler burst into the crowded room, smashed a beer mug to the floor, and pushed forward at the head of his storm troops, brandishing a pistol. In the pandemonium, he jumped on a table and fired a shot into the ceiling. 'National revolution has broken out!' he yelled. 'Farce! South America!' was the response from a few wags, who were promptly beaten up. The new Hitler style of politics had indisputably arrived. Today, *Hilton City Hotel* stands on the site and there is no plaque commemorating the putsch.

replaced by hardline communists. After fierce and bloody fighting with the Freikorps, the Bavarian Red Army was defeated, and the short-lived independent republic of Bavaria was crushed.

Hitler's Munich

Adolf Hitler had first been drawn to Munich by its cultural ambience, but he remained immune to the innovative tendencies of the avant-garde. His own painting was stolidly academic and attracted no attention. He turned to the clamour of German nationalism, and a chance photograph taken at a rally on Odeonsplatz in August 1914 shows Hitler in the crowd, joyfully greeting news of the declaration of war.

He returned to Munich as a corporal in 1918. It was while working to re-educate soldiers in nationalistic, anti-Marxist ideas at the end of the Bavarian Republic that he joined the Deutsche Arbeiter-Partei. By February 1920, he was able to address two thousand members in the Hofbräuhaus. The association soon became known as the Nationalsozialistische Deutsche Arbeiter-Partei, or

Nazi Party. Its symbol was the swastika. Armed storm troops of the party's Sturm-Abteilung (SA) broke up any opposition political meetings held in Munich.

At a January 1923 meeting, Hitler declared: 'Either the Nazi Party is the German movement of the future, in which case no devil can stop it, or it isn't, in which case it deserves to be destroyed'. Both proved true. By November, the party had 55,000 members and 15,000 storm troops. Hitler then felt strong enough to stage his famous Beer Hall Putsch.

This was intended as a first move in the campaign to force the Bavarian state government to cooperate in a Nazi march on Berlin. The putsch ended in a debacle on Odeonsplatz with Hitler being sent

Illustration of Ludwig I's funeral in Munich by Gaildrau (1868)

to prison, but not before he had twisted the whole affair to his advantage. He ensured that his trial for treason became an indictment of his prosecutors as accomplices of the 'November criminals' who, he said, had stabbed Germany in the back in 1918 with their anti-war movement. Hitler became an instant hero. In prison at nearby Landsberg, he was not required to perform prison duties but instead held political meetings and used his time to write his manifesto, *Mein Kampf*.

Hitler's career took him to Berlin, but the Nazis kept their party headquarters in Munich at the Brown House (named after the colour of their shirts). Brighter spirits of the time, including the whimsical comedian Karl Valentin and a fan of his, the dramatist Bertolt Brecht, also made their home in Munich.

In 1935, Munich became known as the 'Capital of the (Nazi) Movement'. Its status at the vanguard was confirmed in June 1938, when the central synagogue was looted, presaging the *Kristallnacht* (Night of Broken Glass) rampage five months later, when Jewish premises across Germany were attacked.

In September of that year, Munich also became a symbol of the ignominious appeasement decisions by Britain and France. In Munich's Führerbau, a meeting took place between prime ministers Neville Chamberlain and Edouard Daladier, during which they negotiated the dismemberment of Czechoslovakia with Hitler and Mussolini. Later, Chamberlain obtained a signed piece of paper from the Führer, a guarantee he claimed of 'peace in our time'.

War and peace

Large-scale resistance to the Nazis was not possible in wartime Munich, but there were voices of dissent including the *Weisse Rose* student movement, which distributed anti-Hitler leaflets at the university. But the founders, Hans and Sophie Scholl and Christoph Probst, were guillotined on 22 February 1943.

A total of 71 air raids hit the city during World War II, killing six thousand and wounding 16,000. Attacks were most intense in 1944, heavily damaging the Frauenkirche, St Peter's and St Michael's churches, and parts of the Residenz and Alte Pinakothek. The city still remembers the dark days of the Third Reich and is not afraid to talk about it.

Postwar reconstruction was a triumph of hard work and loyal attachment to the great traditions of Munich's past. Monuments, palaces and churches were restored with care. Open to the arts and good living, Munich expanded and became Germany's third-largest city, welcoming Berliners and refugees. The city continues to build on its international reputation as a city of culture, with a year-round programme of performing arts.

The Nazi Party's infamous 'Beer Hall Putsch' at Marienplatz in November 1923

Chronology

8th century Small settlement of Benedictine monks gives the site its name.
1158 Henry the Lion sets up toll station for the salt trade from Salzburg.
1180 Emperor Frederick Barbarossa seizes Munich from Henry and hands the city over to the Wittelsbach family.
1328 Duke Ludwig IV becomes Holy Roman Emperor, and his court is established in Munich.
1348 Black Death brings devastation to Munich.
15th century A period of prosperity – transit point for trade from Venice.
1632 Swedish armies invade Munich during the Thirty Years' War.
1638 Mariensäule erected on Marienplatz.
1704–1714 Austrian occupation of Munich.
1742 Hungarian hussars take over the city.
1789 American Benjamin Thompson develops the Englischer Garten.
1805 Napoleon visits Munich.
1806 Napoleon raises Bavaria to status of kingdom.
1826 Ludwig I lays the foundation stone for the Alte Pinakothek.
1845 Bavarian King Ludwig II is born.
1886 Ludwig II found drowned in Lake Starnberg close to Schloss Berg.
1918 The Bavarian Republic declared. Ludwig III flees.
1919 Kurt Eisner, leader of a short-lived socialist regime, is assassinated.
1923 Adolf Hitler stages his famous 'Beer Hall Putsch'.
1935 Munich named capital of the Nazi Movement.
1939–1945 World War II: 71 air raids on the city, killing six thousand.
1972 Munich hosts the Summer Olympic Games.
2002 Pinakothek der Moderne opens. Germany adopts the euro.
2006 Jewish Museum of Munich opens at St-Jakobs-Platz.

Hitler and Mussolini in Munich on June 18, 1940

2009 Museum Brandhorst opens.
2012 Munich celebrates two hundred years of the beer garden. Artworks stolen during the Nazi period are rediscovered.
2015 Germany welcomes up to a million refugees displaced by the Syrian civil war, with around 90,000 settling in Bavaria.
2017 Angela Merkel – Germany's first female leader – wins a fourth term as chancellor in federal elections.
2021 Angela Merkel steps down after a historic sixteen years as chancellor. Olaf Scholz takes the reins, steering a coalition with the Greens and the Free Democrats.
2025 Conservative leader Friedrich Merz becomes chancellor, helming a Christian Democratic Union (CDU) government in coalition with the Socialist Democratic Party (SDP). Stricter border controls are immediately effective.

The Neue Rathaus in Marienplatz

Places

Munich has two enormous assets as far as the visitor is concerned. First, a large majority of the city's museums, monuments, palaces and churches are clustered in the Innenstadt (inner city), ripe for exploration on foot. Second, Munich's public transport, spanning buses, trams, underground (*U-Bahn*) and suburban trains (*S-Bahn*), brings all the other sights within easy reach so there is no need for a car.

Munich long ago expanded beyond the narrow confines of its medieval boundaries, and the old city wall long since disappeared. However, the remains of three gates survive, marking out the perimeter of the inner city – Isartor, Karlstor and Sendlinger Tor – as well as Odeonsplatz, a rendezvous for salt traders setting off in the fourteenth century for Northern Germany. Ever since Munich's earliest beginnings, however, Marienplatz has been at the heart of it all.

In and around Marienplatz

Highlights

- **Altes Rathaus and Neues Rathaus**, see pages 40 and 41
- **Frauenkirche**, see page 42
- **Alter Peter**, see page 43
- **Viktualienmarkt**, see page 44
- **Alter Hof and the Hofbräuhaus**, see page 45

Until the middle of the nineteenth century, **Marienplatz** ❶ was the location of the wheat market. The square was the obvious site for the town hall, and the place where criminals were hanged. It was also the scene of the most extravagant wedding Munich has ever seen – that of Duke Wilhelm V to Renata of Lorraine in 1568. It was the inevitable choice for the central interchange of the U-Bahn and S-Bahn system in 1972.

BEST PLACES TO TAKE PHOTOS

A treat for the eyes and the camera, the Wittelsbach Residenz (see page 53) is the greatest monument of Max-Joseph, the fourth Max-Joseph of the Wittelsbach dynasty. The Königsbau, bordering the Residenz square on the north side, is the best spot to set up for photos, with multiple attractions and angles.

A slice of the English countryside in Munich, the lovely Englischer Garten (see page 71) is a wonderful expanse of greenery and landscaping. To capture the best photos of the Englischer Garten, aim to get set up as close as you can to the Greek temple.

Marienplatz today forms part of an attractive pedestrian zone and is home to the **Mariensäule** (Column of the Virgin Mary), erected in 1638 by Maximilian I in gratitude for the town's deliverance from the Plague after its defeat by the Swedes during the Thirty Years' War. At the base of the monument are a basilisk, dragon, serpent and lion – representing plague, hunger, heresy and war – each being vanquished by heroic cherubs. On the top of the obelisk is the gilded figure of Mary, who watches over Munich. Holding Jesus in her left arm and a sceptre in her right, she is a reminder of Munich's religious foundation. The square also contains the nineteenth-century **Fischbrunnen**. Young butchers used to leap into the bronze fountain at the end of their apprenticeship, but today the tradition is kept up only by Fasching (Carnival) revellers or raucous football fans.

Two town halls

At the eastern end of Marienplatz, the picturesque **Altes Rathaus** ❷ (Old Town Hall) is an example of Munich's efforts to rebuild, rather than replace, the remnants of its venerable history. The dove-grey facade, amber-tiled steeple and graceful spires of this Gothic-style edifice capture the spirit of the fifteenth-century edifice designed by Jörg von Halsbach (alias Jörg Ganghofer), though it isn't an exact replica. In any case, with the addition over the centuries of a Baroque onion-shaped cupola and then an overzealous attempt to replicate Gothic features, the building that was destroyed by Allied bombs was likely further from the original than what you see today. Next to the main building, the clock tower shelters the **Spielzeugmuseum** (Toy Museum; charge). Fascinating collections, ranging from antique train sets to zoo animals, are spread over four floors linked by a spiral staircase.

The Old Town Hall contains a banqueting hall, but the daily business of city government takes place at the **Neues Rathaus** (New Town Hall) on the northern side of the square. This is a fine example of nineteenth-century Neo-Gothic architecture, proud and self-assertive, with a facade elaborately decorated with the statues of kings, princes and dukes, saints, allegorical figures and characters from Munich folklore. The tower is 85m (260ft) high; its main attraction, apart from the splendid view (lift to the top; charge) is the 43-bell **Glockenspiel** (carillon), which puts on two shows daily, at 11am and noon, plus 5pm in summer. Two groups of figures appear, one group re-enacting the tournament held during the wedding of Duke Wilhelm V and Renata of Lorraine and the other, underneath, recreating the cooper's dance

The Glockenspiel

(*Schäfflertanz*), which was performed to cheer up the surviving population after the plague of 1517. In the evening, at 9pm, a night watchman with lantern blows his horn and an angel of peace blesses the little Munich monk (*Münchner Kindl*).

Frauenkirche

Now head along Weinstrasse (from the west side of Marienplatz) and left along Sporerstrasse to reach Frauenplatz and the enormous Domkirche zu Unserer Lieben Frau (Cathedral Church of Our Lady), usually referred to simply as the **Frauenkirche** ❸. With its twin brick towers crowned by bulbous domes (99m/325ft high), this church has always been Munich's defining landmark. An austere, unadorned Gothic structure, it was built between 1468 and 1488 by Jörg von Halsbach (aka Jörg Ganghofer). The Italian Renaissance domes are a 1524 addition.

The tower of the Alter Peter

The stark interior was reconstructed from the rubble of World War II bombardments – a truly heroic work of restoration. The original Gothic windows in the choir, stored safely away during the war, give an impression of the church's former glory. Fine sculptures of the Apostles and Prophets also escaped destruction and adorn the choir as before. They were created by Erasmus Grasser in 1502. Dating from 1483 a fine altarpiece by Friedrich Pacher, the *Baptism of Christ*, hangs in the north chapel. It is flanked by Jan Polack's panels depicting Jesus on the Mount of Olives and his arrest, crucifixion and burial. Notice, too, the seventeenth-century funerary monument of Emperor Ludwig the Bavarian, who died in 1347.

It's possible to ascend the **South Tower** by stairs or a lift for a unique view of the city from the top windows (charge).

NOTES

In addition to its twin towers, the Frauenkirche is known for its 'Devil's Footprint'. Jörg von Halsbach made a pact with Satan that in return for the money to complete the church, he would design it without any visible windows. This was but an illusion, however, there being just one point near the entrance from which no windows could be seen. Thus deceived, the devil stamped his foot in fury; both imprint and illusion can be seen to this day.

Alter Peter

Looming over the south side of Marienplatz, but not quite on the square itself, **St Peter's** ❹ is Munich's oldest church, dating from before the foundation of the city itself in 1158, hence its nickname Alter Peter – Old Peter. The original structure gave way to a building in the Romanesque style, succeeded in time by a Gothic church that boasted a twin-steepled tower. Everything but the tower was obliterated in the great fire of 1327, and a new Gothic edifice went up. This was remodelled along Renaissance lines in the seventeenth century, and a new tower with a single steeple was created. Destroyed in the war, St Peter's has been faithfully reconstructed. It's well worth climbing the 306 steps to the observation balcony at the top for the stunning views over the city.

Viktualienmarkt

The crowning piece of the light, bright interior is the **high altar** glorifying Peter and the fathers of the Church. It was carefully restored from the remnants of the eighteenth-century original, inspired by Bernini's altar for St Peter's in Rome. Egid Quirin Asam (see page 50) was the designer of the ensemble, incorporating Erasmus Grasser's *St Peter*.

The gilded wood figures of the Church fathers are the masterly work of Egid Quirin. Leading up to the altar are splendid Rococo choir stalls. You'll also see five of Jan Polack's Late Gothic paintings that once adorned the altar. They show Peter healing the lame, enthroned, at sea, in prison and on the cross.

Also from the Late Gothic period is the Schrenk Altar, a fine early-fifteenth-century sandstone relief of the Crucifixion and the Day of Judgment.

Viktualienmarkt

Just behind St Peter's, at the other side of Rosenstrasse, the **Viktualienmarkt** ❺ (www.viktualienmarkt-muenchen.de) is one of the most colourful locations in Munich and a magnet for all who love food. The city's central market has been trading here since 1807. Stroll around the enticing stalls piled high with local cheeses, fragrant spices, home-made breads, meats, fruit and vegetables.

The cheerful atmosphere makes it the ideal place for annual performances of the Marketwomen's Dance, held on Shrove Tuesday. It's also the scene of a series of lively celebrations around the flower-bedecked maypole.

Adjacent to the Viktualienmarkt is **Heiliggeistkirche** (Church of the Holy Spirit; www.heilig-geist-muenchen.de). This fourteenth-century Gothic structure was extensively altered to suit the Baroque tastes of the 1720s. The two styles come together perfectly in the **Marienaltar** – a lovely wooden sculpture of 1450, the *Hammerthaler Muttergottes* (Hammerthal Mother of God) originally from the Lake Tegernsee monastery, set in a gilded Baroque frame. The high altar preserves a fine pair of *Adoring Angels* from 1730 by Johann Georg Greiff.

Inside the Alter Hof

Alter Hof and the Hofbräuhaus

Coming out of the church, duck down little Burgstrasse past the Altes Rathaus. Pause at No. 5 to admire the **Hofer** restaurant (see page 123). One of only a handful of Gothic houses still remaining in Munich, this was once the home of the town clerk. Built in about 1550, it has a neatly restored leafy courtyard and a staircase tower.

Continue along Burgstrasse to the **Alter Hof**, Munich's old royal residence, which was originally built in

1255 by Ludwig the Stern in the then northeastern part of the city. It was designed as a defence against foreign invaders as well as the city's own unruly burghers, but was eventually superseded by the Residenz (see page 53).

The buildings suffered more at the hands of nineteenth-century urban developers than during the twentieth-century bombing. However, as you pass through the gates into the courtyard, you'll see that parts of the complex have been superbly restored. The reconstructed Burgtor (City Gate) and quaint Affenturm (Monkey Tower) in the west wing recapture the atmosphere of the Wittelsbachs' first Munich residence as it was in the fifteenth century. The heraldic painting on the tower came to light during the 1960s.

The Hofbräuhaus

Turn right on Pfisterstrasse to Platzl (Little Square), the site of a building of no great architectural distinction but one of Munich's greatest attractions, the **Hofbräuhaus** ❻ (Royal Brewery; www.hofbraeuhaus.de) beer hall. Duke Wilhelm V founded a brewery in the Alter Hof in 1589 to dodge paying the high prices for imported beer from Hanover.

Beer has always been just as popular among the aristocracy as with the common people of Bavaria. It replaced wine as the staple alcoholic beverage after the

KARL VALENTIN

Although little known outside Germany, Karl Valentin was regarded by connoisseurs as a comic genius equal to Charlie Chaplin. While resident in Munich in the early 1920s, the dramatist Bertolt Brecht went almost every night to watch Valentin's portrayal of the clownish, working-class characters of peasant origin who were so peculiar to the city.

Munich's artists and intellectuals loved Valentin's wacky, surreal logic. One of his most celebrated sketches portrayed an attempt to house birds in an aquarium and fish in a birdcage.

Bavarian vineyards were ravaged by the cruel winters of the thirteenth and fourteenth centuries, making way for the sturdier hop and barley crops.

The brewery was first established in the royal bathhouse and moved to these more spacious quarters in 1644. The Hofbräuhaus itself was built in 1896, after the brewery was transferred to the other side of the River Isar. It soon became the most prestigious of Munich's many political beer-hall arenas. In November 1921, Hitler's storm troops first gained notoriety in what became known as the *Saalschlacht im Hofbräuhaus* (Battle of the Hofbräuhaus). Today, the huge space, with its long tables and oompah music, is a magnet for tourists.

To the city gates

Highlights

- **Eastwards to Isartor**, see page 48
- **Münchner Stadtmuseum**, see page 48
- **Jüdisches Zentrum**, see page 49
- **Asamkirche**, see page 50
- **Fussgängerzone**, see page 50
- **Karlsplatz and around**, see page 52

Beyond Marienplatz and its immediate surroundings, there are many more sights to discover in Munich's Innenstadt (Inner City). They're reached by following the main historic arteries leading from Marienplatz to the old city gates.

Eastwards to Isartor

Just south of the Hofbräuhaus, is another venerable Munich institution, the **Weisses Bräuhaus** (www.weisses-brauhaus-tal.de), the beer hall/restaurant of the Schneider Brewery, known for its *Weissbier* (wheat beer). Press eastwards along Tal to the **Isartor**, the only city gate that retains its original fourteenth-century dimensions. Put up in the days when the Bavarian Duke Ludwig IV was Holy Roman Emperor, the gate is splashed with a later fresco dating from 1835 showing him returning triumphantly from victory over the Habsburgs.

The Ohel Jakob Synagogue on St-Jakobs-Platz

Münchner Stadtmuseum

The walk to Sendlinger Tor takes you past the municipal museum and through the busy shopping area of Sendlinger Strasse. From the southeast corner of Marienplatz, follow Rindermarkt past St Peter's Church. The street soon widens into a square, the centre of which holds the **Rinderbrunnen** (cattle fountain), designed by Joseph Henselmann.

From here cut across Rosental and into St-Jakobs-Platz, home to the excellent **Münchner Stadtmuseum** ❼ (Munich City Museum; www.muenchner-stadtmuseum.de; charge). Closed for long-term renovations until 2031, the main exhibition looks at the Bavarian capital's past through a series of themes, periods and personalities.

Asamkirche interior

All aspects of the city's story are dealt with, from the Frauenkirche and Schäfflertanz to Nymphenburg porcelain and the rise of the Nazis. A must-visit when it reopens.

Jüdisches Zentrum

In the centre of the square, the **Jüdisches Zentrum am Jakobsplatz** ❽ (Jakobsplatz Jewish Centre) comprises an austere huddle of cuboid buildings – the Ohel Jakob Synagogue, the Jewish Community Centre and the **Jüdisches Museum** (www.juedisches-museum-muenchen.de; charge).

Guided tours allow visitors to see the synagogue, while the museum's permanent exhibition, Voices_Places_Times, regales the history of the Jewish community in and around Munich through a series of installations. A major focus is directed towards Jewish festivals past and present and contemporary aspects of the religion.

The centre hosts a wide range of cultural events, including concerts and lectures.

Asamkirche

From the Jewish Museum cross Oberanger and walk up the short Hermann-Sack-Strasse to arrive in Sendlinger Strasse. Amid the shops on the right-hand side (No. 62) rises the famous Church of St John Nepomuk, better known as the **Asamkirche** ❾ after its creator, the Bavarian architect and sculptor Egid Quirin Asam (1692–1750). This master of late Baroque illusion had wanted to build his own private church here but was forced to make it accessible to the public after fierce local resistance. The foundation stone was laid in 1733, and the consecration took place in 1746. Asam was assisted in the design by his brother, Cosmas Damian, who specialised in fresco painting. The result is one of the most astonishing achievements of Bavarian Baroque. The interior is a theatrical masterpiece of sculpture, decoration and light; the **high altar** leads the eye up to a large Crucifixion dominated by a representation of God the Father wearing the papal crown.

Next door is the **Asamhaus**, where Egid Quirin lived. It was built at the same time as the church, and again with the assistance of Cosmas Damian. It's worth admiring the intricate facade. Secure in their Catholic faith, the Asam brothers happily mixed pagan and Christian figures in their decorative schemes. At the end of Sendlinger Strasse, only two hexagonal towers remain from the fourteenth-century **Sendlinger Tor**.

Fussgängerzone

West of Marienplatz, Kaufingerstrasse leads into Neuhauser Strasse; together they form the longest section of Munich's **Fussgängerzone** (pedestrian precinct), busy with shoppers and popular with summertime buskers. At the corner of Neuhauser Strasse and Augustinerstrasse is the former Augustinian church;

in Napoleonic times it became a customs house and much later, in 1966, a museum of hunting and fishing, the **Deutsches Jagd- und Fischereimuseum** (www.jagd-fischerei-museum.de; charge). Fronted by a wild boar in bronze, the collection will fascinate hunters, anglers and children alike.

Further along Neuhauser Strasse is the sixteenth-century **St Michael's**, an Italian Renaissance church with Baroque overtones (the first of its kind in Germany), designed by the Dutch architect Friedrich Sustris. St Michael's epitomises the combative spirit of the Counter-Reformation, and it is fitting that the Wittelsbach dukes and German emperors, the secular defenders of the faith, are depicted on the gabled facade. Above the entrance, third

The elegant Wittelsbacher Brunnen

figure from the right, stands the church's founder, Duke Wilhelm V (with a model of the church in his hand). The interior is a gigantic Renaissance hall, 20m (66ft) wide, with a barrel-vaulted ceiling; at the time of its construction, only St Peter's in Rome was larger.

The nearby fountain, the **Richard Strauss-Brunnen**, with its sculpture group from the opera *Salome*, commemorates Munich's best-known musician, the composer of world-famous operas, lieder and tone poems.

Karlsplatz and environs

Karlstor, a city gate dating from the fourteenth century, links Neuhauser Strasse to the busy Karlsplatz, which is popularly

The Nationaltheater

known as Stachus after an innkeeper named Eustachius Föderl. Stachus conceals a veritable city of underground shops, which stretches from the exit of the U- and S-Bahn station.

Walk north to Lenbachplatz and you'll find the city's loveliest fountain, the late-nineteenth-century **Wittelsbacher Brunnen**, which was built in neo-Baroque style by Adolf von Hildebrand. Pacellistrasse, to the east of Lenbachplatz, takes you past the Baroque facade of the **Dreifaltigkeitskirche** (Trinity Church). In 1704 a young girl, Anna Maria Lindmayr, dreamt that Munich would be invaded and destroyed unless a new church were constructed. Sure enough, the next year, during the War of the Spanish Succession, Austrian soldiers arrived. Although work on the Dreifaltigkeitskirche did not begin until 1711, the town was saved from destruction.

The Residenz and surroundings

Highlights

- **Residenzmuseum and Treasury**, see page 55
- **Cuvilliés-Theater**, see page 56
- **Odeonsplatz**, see page 57
- **Ludwigstrasse**, see page 60

Max-Joseph-Platz is named after the king whose statue sits in the centre: the fourth Max-Joseph of the Wittelsbach dynasty and the first, thanks to Napoleon, to be king. The statue was built alongside the greatest monument of Max-Joseph's family, the Wittelsbach **Residenz** ❿. In 1385 the citizenry revolted, driving the dukes to construct safer lodgings than the Alter Hof. More than five centuries later, in 1918, another group of rebellious citizens pounded on the Residenz doors during the revolution that resulted in the short-lived Bavarian Socialist Republic. The Wittelsbachs were forced to move out once again, this time for good.

Looking along Viscardigasse towards the Residenz

The largely reconstructed Residenz, now a museum, reveals just how wealthy the Bavarian principality grew to be. Successive members of the Wittelsbach dynasty expanded the original stronghold to create a complex of palaces around seven courtyards. The Königsbau or King's Tract, bordering the square on the north side, was only built between 1826 and 1835, on the instructions of Ludwig I to house his apartments. Ludwig's architect, Leo von Klenze, adapted the designs of Karl von Fischer to create a heavily rusticated facade with 21 bays in the style of the Florentine Palazzo Pitti.

Before entering the museum through the large central doors, note three other buildings on the square. Opposite stands the Neoclassical former **Hauptpostamt**, or Main Post Office, also designed by Klenze. Rebuilt in 1963, the **Nationaltheater**, Munich's opera house, bounds the east side of the square. It is a copy of the 1818 original, a Greek-temple design by Karl von Fischer (first rebuilt by Leo von Klenze after a fire in 1825). Sandwiched between the Residenz and the opera house is the **Residenztheater** (www.residenztheater.de), which was built between 1948 and 1951 by Karl Hocheder in place of the Cuvilliés-Theater (see page 57).

Max-Joseph-Platz also marks the beginning of **Maximilianstrasse**, Munich's most elegant avenue, which stretches away towards the River Isar and the brooding presence beyond of the Maximilianeum (see page 75).

Residenzmuseum and Treasury

The **Residenzmuseum** ⓫ (www.residenz-muenchen.de) can be visited independently or as part of a guided tour. There's a huge amount to see in the 112 rooms, halls and galleries, in addition to the ten rooms of the Schatzkammer (Treasure Chamber). The highlights include:

Ahnengalerie (Gallery of the Ancestors). Acquaint yourself with a mere 121 of the Wittelsbachs, starting with Duke Theodor, who lived around AD 700.

Antiquarium. Designed by Friedrich Sustris for Duke Albrecht V in 1558, this is the largest and most beautiful Renaissance hall north of the Alps. The room takes its name from the sixteenth-century busts of ancient Greek and Roman leaders on display.

Porcelain collections. This prodigious array of French, English and German porcelain includes Meissen, from near Dresden, as well as local pieces produced in Nymphenburg. Japanese and Chinese porcelain and superb lacquer work form part of a separate exhibit.

Reiche Zimmer. Together, these State Rooms provide the most outstanding example of Rococo decor in Germany. Cuvilliés designed them in 1729, and his jewel among jewels was the Grüne Galerie (Green Gallery). The Spiegelkabinett (Cabinet of Mirrors), Miniaturenkabinett and Chinesisches Kabinett are equally fascinating.

Hofkapelle and Reiche Kapelle. Of these intimate chapels, the first was originally set aside for common courtiers, while the second was for the exclusive use of the Wittelsbachs.

Grottenhof. Designed by Sustris in 1581, this is perhaps the most elegant courtyard in the Residenz, distinguished by the graceful arcade along the eastern side and by Hubert Gerhard's fine bronze Perseus fountain set in the middle. The Grottenwand,

The Cuvilliés-Theater

or Grotto Wall (with a fountain in an alcove), gives the courtyard its name. A statue of Mercury is flanked by enslaved Nubians, fish-tailed satyrs, nymphs and parrots, and the ensemble is encrusted with thousands of mussel, scallop and winkle shells.

Schatzkammer (Treasury). A separate exhibition (extra charge) displays the dynasty's spectacular collection of jewellery, gold, silver, crystal and enamelware, amassed over the course of a thousand years. One of the earliest of the Wittelsbach heirlooms is a communion goblet dating from about 890, known as the Arnulfziborium (Arnolph's Ciborium).

The courtyards and Cuvilliés–Theater

Apart from the Grottenhof, all the courtyards of the Residenz can be visited free of charge by entering the complex via the older

Maximilian Residenz, whose early seventeenth-century facade runs along Residenzstrasse. The most attractive courtyard is the **Brunnenhof**, or Fountain Court, to the right of the entrance, which was built in the shape of a long, stretched octagon in 1620. The centrepiece Wittelsbach fountain features Duke Otto von Wittelsbach with four mermen symbolising Bavaria's most important rivers at his feet.

From the Brunnenhof you can enter the enchanting **Cuvilliés-Theater** ⓬ (separate admission). This Rococo gem was originally located where the present Residenztheater stands and found its present location after World War II, when the Brunnenhof layout was reconstructed. Its architect, François de Cuvilliés the Elder, was from the Spanish Netherlands, and the theatre is tiny, seating just 450 people. But its sense of festive intimacy turns every performance into a cosy gala. The four-tiered auditorium basks in gilded decor with hosts of Greek nymphs, gods and goddesses, and, with marvellous incongruity, an Native American girl with bow and arrow. The acoustics are warm and golden – perfectly suited to the works by Mozart that have been performed here for the past two hundred years.

NOTES

The Cuvilliés-Theater owes its survival to planning and foresight. In 1943, its stucco ornamentation and sculptures were dismantled. Some 30,000 pieces were carried away and stashed in the vaults of various castles around Munich. Only six weeks later the theatre was gutted by firebombs. However, fifteen years elapsed before all the pieces were brought out of hiding and reassembled.

Odeonsplatz

Residenzstrasse leads out into **Odeonsplatz**, which forms a link between the inner city and Maxvorstadt and the university to the north. If you're coming from Marienplatz, you can

LEO VON KLENZE

In the early nineteenth century Munich was transformed from a simple residence city into an international centre of art and culture. This is largely down to the collaboration of two men, King Ludwig I, avid art collector and fan of antiquity, and Leo von Klenze, his star architect. Klenze, who was also a noted painter and writer, created a glittering array of Neoclassical buildings that cities even twice the size of Munich would have been proud to possess. His projects included the Glyptothek (1815), the rebuild of the Nationaltheater (1823), the Alte Pinakothek (1826), the Königsbau of the Residenz (1826) and the Hauptpostamt (1834). Klenze, along with Friedrich von Gärtner, the sculptor Ludwig Schwanthaler and the painter Peter Cornelius, also gave shape to the Maxvorstadt between Munich and Schwabing, with the elegant Ludwigstrasse as the main axis. He was active outside Munich too, most notably with his work on the New Hermitage in St Petersburg (1839).

also stroll along **Theatinerstrasse**, which is pleasantly pedestrianised and lined by cafés with outdoor tables. Also look out for the entrance to the **Fünf Höfe** (www.fuenfhoefe.de), a high-class shopping arcade featuring top designer names.

Odeonsplatz is dominated on its western flank by the twin towers and dome of the **Theatinerkirche** ⓭ (www.theatinerkirche.de). This splendid Italian Baroque church was built between 1663 and 1668 by two Italian architects, Agostino Barelli and Enrico Zuccalli. The facade was completed later by Cuvilliés. Perhaps because the church was created to celebrate the birth of a baby boy to Princess Henriette Adelaide, a feeling of jubilation animates its rich decoration – with sprigs of ornamental vines, acanthus leaves and rosettes in the most spirited Italian Baroque style, and grey-and-white stucco embellishments in the cupola. Notice, as well, the triumphant pulpit, the high altar and, to the left, the Cajetan altar. This last was dedicated to St Cajetan, founder of the Theatine Order.

Just across the street, facing Odeonsplatz, is the **Feldherrnhalle** (Hall of the Generals), a nineteenth-century monument to several Bavarian military leaders, including the Belgian-born Count Johann Tilly (a hero in the Thirty Years' War) and Prince Karl-Philipp von Wrede, who achieved victory over the French in 1814. Less gloriously, it was the rendezvous for Nazi storm troops in Hitler's unsuccessful putsch of 1923 and was subsequently a focus for marches commemorating the event. Reinforcing the Italian atmosphere of the area, though with less of a light touch, the building is modelled after the Loggia dei Lanzi in Florence.

At the east side of the square an archway leads through to the Italian Renaissance-style **Hofgarten** (Court Garden), restored and

The Glyptothek on Königsplatz

replanted with the chestnut trees, flowerbeds and fountains specified in the original seventeenth-century plan. In the centre stands a twelve-sided temple dedicated to Diana, topped by a bronze statue of Bavaria. The arcades that flank the garden house art galleries and cafés are decorated with frescoes of historic scenes featuring the Wittelsbachs.

Ludwigstrasse

Odeonsplatz gives way to **Ludwigstrasse**, which stretches north towards Schwabing (see page 69). This grand avenue of Neoclassical buildings, leading into what at the time was nothing but open countryside, was the most eccentric project of the crown prince (later king) Ludwig I. He commissioned the buildings as far as Theresienstrasse to the prolific Leo von Klenze; beyond that, Friedrich von Gärtner took over with his designs for the Bavarian State Library and the University. An equestrian statue of Ludwig I stands at the beginning of his street, outside Klenze's noble **Leuchtenberg Palais**.

The Museum Quarter

Highlights

- **Königsplatz**, see below
- **Lenbachhaus**, see page 63
- **Kunstareal München**, see page 64

Königsplatz

To the northwest of the inner city, beyond the Alter Botanischer Garten, **Königsplatz** ⓮ represents a convergence of the noblest and basest aspirations arising from the past several hundred years of Munich's history. When Ludwig I was still crown prince, he visualised the square as a second Acropolis, a vast open space surrounded by Classical temples. There was no particular reason for the choice of this site (no junction of roads, for example). Ludwig simply overrode the customary demands of urban planning and soon men were working on widening the stately Brienner Strasse, the street that took the royal family from the Residenz to Nymphenburg Palace.

With Leo von Klenze working as his architect, Ludwig converted the square into a grass-covered, tree-lined haven of tranquillity. A hundred years later, Hitler cut down the trees and paved over the grass for the troops and armoured cars of his military parades. (The pompous Nazi Ehrentempel, or Temple of Honour, which stood at the eastern end of the square, was deliberately blown up by the Allied military engineers in 1945.) Today, at last, Königsplatz has returned to its original serenity, and the pastoral greenery is back.

The Aeginates in the Glyptothek

The U-Bahn station brings you out beside the **Propyläen** (Propylaeum), modelled after the entranceway to the Acropolis in Athens. Unlike the original, this splendid monument to Ludwig's sublime imperviousness to functional considerations does not lead anywhere, for it closes off Königsplatz, rather than providing access to the square. Despite the Doric columns, it's not even authentically Greek, since the central

Lenbachhaus art gallery, in an 1880s Florentine Renaissance-style villa

gateway is flanked by two Egyptian-style pylons. The adorning friezes show the Wittelsbachs' special attachment to all things Greek: representations of the Greek war of liberation from the Turks, and of the Greek people paying homage to Ludwig's son Otto when he was made their king in 1832.

Situated on the south side of Königsplatz, the **Staatliche Antikensammlungen** (Classical Art Collections; www.antike-am-koenigsplatz.mwn.de; charge) appears somewhat clumsy with its Corinthian columns set on an excessively elevated pedestal. The displays include a beautiful series of Greek vases and urns, and, above all, the highly prized collection of Etruscan gold and silver curated by James Loeb. This German-American benefactor is known to students and scholars through the famous Loebs Classical Library of Greek and Latin texts.

Just across the square, its companion building, the **Glyptothek** 15 (www.antike-am-koenigsplatz.mwn.de) was designed in 1815 by von Klenze to display Ludwig I's large collection of Greek and Roman sculpture – the first building to be planned for use as a public museum. Some 160 pieces, procured on the orders of the king, found a home in the massive, Ionic-columned edifice. The Glyptothek's greatest treasure is the sculpture from the gables of the Temple of Aphaia, found on the Greek island of Aegina.

These well-preserved friezes, the *Aeginates*, have been dated to 505 BC (west gable) and 485 BC (east gable) and feature warriors with shields, fighting to defend the island's patron goddess. Other works of major importance include the *Apollo of Tenea, a Medusa*, the goddess of peace Irene and the *Barberini Faun* (named after a seventeenth-century Italian family of Classicists).

Lenbachhaus

Before crossing Königsplatz completely, retrace your steps through the Propyläen and walk over the road to the **Lenbachhaus** 16 (www.lenbachhaus.de; charge) on Luisenstrasse. This elegant ochre-coloured villa, built in the 1880s in the style of the Florentine Renaissance, was originally the residence of Franz von Lenbach, a wealthy art collector.

Expanded and redesigned in 2013 by British architect Norman Foster, today it shelters an excellent art gallery featuring Munich paintings from the Gothic period to the present day. The most important and popular collections are those from the nineteenth and twentieth centuries, including the largest collection of Wassily Kandinsky paintings in Germany, in addition to canvases by Franz Marc, Gabriele Münter, Alexej von Jawlensky, August Macke and Paul Klee. These artists were the members of Munich's pre-World War I *Blaue Reiter* (Blue Rider) school of painting. The name derives from a blue-and-black horseman drawn by Kandinsky for an almanac in 1912. Horses were also a

NOTES

When the U-Bahn at Königsplatz was built in the late 1970s, an enormous unused space between ground level and the station platforms was created. In 1994 this was converted for use as an art gallery; run as an annexe to the Municipal Gallery in the Lenbachhaus, the Kunstbau hosts prestigious temporary modern art exhibitions.

dominant feature of Franz Marc's work. The Lenbachhaus became a gallery for the *Blaue Reiter* collection in 1929. Alongside these works the displays include works by Picasso, Braque, Dalí, the German Expressionists, Joseph Beuys and a distinguished array of contemporary Americans.

Kunstareal München

Leave Königsplatz heading north along Arcisstrasse and cross Gabelsberger Strasse to arrive at the Alte Pinakothek, the first of the major museums that make up what is referred to as the Kunstareal München (Munich Art Area; www.kunstareal.de). Visit on Sundays when most museums charge a symbolic €1 admission.

The Neue Pinakothek

Alte Pinakothek

Devoted to works from the fourteenth to the eighteenth centuries, the **Alte Pinakothek** ⓱ (www.pinakothek.de; charge) shelters some of the world's finest European paintings. It was commissioned by Ludwig I to house the royal art collections, which had been acquired over the centuries by various dukes, electors and Wittelsbach kings. The acquisitions of Ludwig himself form a significant portion of the curation.

Albrecht Dürer's 'Self-portrait with a Fur Coat', Alte Pinakothek

Ludwig chose Leo von Klenze to provide a design for a monumental museum in the style of an Italian Renaissance palace. Ludwig himself laid the foundation stone on 7 April 1826, Raphael's birthday. It was badly damaged in the war, though reconstruction in 1958 preserved the spacious layout of galleries and introduced some excellent lighting.

The Alte Pinakothek is renowned for its early Dutch as well as early German Old Masters. The latter includes Albrecht Dürer's famous *Self Portrait in a Fur Coat* (1500), heralding the arrival of the humanistic spirit of Italy's Renaissance in the medieval north, and his *Four Apostles*, which seems to reflect the turbulent times when the Reformation swept through Northern Europe. Another outstanding German piece is the *Altarpiece of the Church Fathers* (*Kirchenväteraltar*), painted in about 1483 by Michael Pacher. Don't

Pinakothek der Moderne, Europe's largest museum of art and design

miss Albrecht Altdorfer's *Alexanderschlacht* (1529), which portrays Alexander's victory over Darius of Persia. The thousands of soldiers make this a miniaturist masterpiece.

The scope and quality of the Flemish collection is unique, including as it does one of the world's finest collections of paintings by Peter Paul Rubens. His works, including the *Great Last Judgement* and the *Rape of the Daughters of Leucippus*, hang on the first floor. The Alte Pinakothek is also richly endowed with works by Italian masters: Giotto, Botticelli, Lippi, Ghirlandaio, Perugino, Raphael, Titian, Tintoretto and Tiepolo are all represented, as is Leonardo da Vinci with a small *Madonna with Child* painted when he was only 21. The Dutch are also here with Rembrandt and Franz Hals, and there is Germany's best curation of Spanish paintings, featuring El Greco, Velázquez and Murillo.

Neue Pinakothek

Opposite the Alte Pinakothek is the **Neue Pinakothek** ⓲ (www.pinakothek.de/besuch/neue-pinakothek; charge). The 'New Gallery', currently undergoing renovations until 2030, was also founded by Ludwig I to house his collection of contemporary art; the building was destroyed in World War II, however. This elegant sandstone and granite replacement, designed by Alexander von Branca, opened in 1981. The gallery contains outstanding works of European art and sculpture from the late eighteenth to the beginning of the twentieth century, ranging from the German Romanticism of Caspar David Friedrich to the Austrian *Jugendstil* of Gustav Klimt. The wonderful collection of French impressionists includes works by Monet, Manet, Degas, Pissaro and Renoir; Cézanne, Gauguin and van Gogh stand for the pioneers of the modern age.

Pinakothek der Moderne

Opposite the Alte Pinakothek is the **Pinakothek der Moderne** ⓳ (www.pinakothek.de/en/pinakothek-der-moderne; charge). Opened in 2002, this is the largest museum of art and design in Europe, bringing art, design, architecture and work on paper under one roof in a cutting-edge building designed by Stephan Braunfels.

Art. This world-class collection ranges from the main avant-garde movements of the early twentieth century to contemporary art. Prominent among the displays, and including some of the 'degenerate art' so despised by the Nazis, are works by artists of *Die Brücke* and the *Blaue Reiter*, and by Max Beckman, who is represented with the largest European display of his works. Picasso is also a standout, as are the surrealists Max Ernst, René Magritte and Salvador Dalí.

Design. A fascinating insight into various design schools from the pioneers of modernism to the present day, focusing on themes such as motor vehicles, bentwood furniture and computer culture.

Architecture. Focusing mainly on German architecture, the curation includes

NOTES

When it was opened in 1836, the Alte Pinakothek was the biggest painting gallery in the world. One of the first purpose-built public museums, it was organised around the different schools of art, and the hanging scheme remains largely the same today.

blueprints dating back to the sixteenth century, as well as photographs, models and computer animations. Look out for works by Balthasar Neumann, Leo von Klenze, Erich Mendelsohn and Le Corbusier.

Work on paper. The huge display of prints and drawings is one of the most important in Germany, containing 400,000 works dating from the fifteenth century to the present.

Museum Brandhorst

The **Museum Brandhorst** ⓴ (www.museum-brandhorst.de; charge) lends a spectacular dimension to the Kunstareal, with stunning contemporary pieces by artists like Cy Twombly, Andy Warhol,

The Monopteros

Damian Hirst and Sigmar Polke. The building itself, designed by Sauerbruch Hutton of Berlin, reflects the exquisite art inside, the facade a composition of 36,000 vertical ceramic rods in 23 different colours, with deep tones at the bottom and light pastel shades at the top.

NS-Dokumentationszentrum

The austere edifice of the **NS-Dokumentationszentrum** ㉑ (The Munich Documentation Centre for the History of National Socialism; www.nsdoku.de; free) conceals exhibitions commemorating the atrocities of the Nazi apparatus and its consequences up to contemporary times. The museum was created in 2015 in the very same place of the former NSDAP headquarters.

Schwabing

Highlights

- **Leopoldstrasse**, see page 70
- **Englischer Garten**, see page 71
- **Prinzregentenstrasse**, see page 73

Ludwigstrasse stretches precisely 1km from Odeonsplatz in the south to **Siegestor** (Victory Gate) at its northern end. This triumphal arch was designed for Ludwig I as a monument to the Bavarian army.

Just south of the Siegestor is the **University** and the little square Geschwister-Scholl-Platz, named in memory of the brother and sister who were killed with a guillotine by the Nazis for leading an underground resistance movement of students against Hitler's regime; an impressive memorial exhibition inside the university building commemorates their activities (www.weisse-rose-stiftung.de; free). Across the street, **St Ludwig's**, (www.st-ludwig-muenchen.de; free) is a neo-Romanesque church noted

SCHWABING'S HEYDAY

During Schwabing's heyday at the turn of the twentieth century, artists and writers flocked to this bohemian corner of Munich. Thomas Mann lived here, as did Frank Wedekind and Bertolt Brecht, Wassily Kandinsky and Paul Klee, as well as Franz Marc, Rainer Maria Rilke and symbolist poet Stefan George.

A countess-turned-bohemian, Franziska zu Reventlow chronicled the area's free love, free art and freedom for all in her novels. Schwabing was also home to the biting satirical weekly *Simplicissimus* and to the art magazine *Jugend*, which gave its name to *Jugendstil*, the German version of Art Nouveau.

In 1919, the 'Coffeehouse Anarchists', dramatist Ernst Toller and poet Erich Mühsam, took power after the assassination of the prime minister, Kurt Eisner. For all of six days – until the communists pushed the poets out – Schwabing ruled Bavaria, proclaiming the republic a 'meadow full of flowers'.

for the gigantic painting of the *Last Judgement* in the choir, by Peter Cornelius (1836). It is the world's second-largest fresco – measuring 18m (60ft) by 11m (37ft) – after Michelangelo's in the Sistine Chapel in Rome.

Leopoldstrasse

Siegestor marks the southern boundary of Munich's once-bohemian district of Schwabing. Its main shopping street and promenade, **Leopoldstrasse**, has been commercialised by ice-cream parlours, fast-food outlets and bars, but the more idyllic, older part of Schwabing can be discovered easily in the side roads that shoot off to the English Garden – Werneckstrasse, for example, or Nikolaiplatz. Ainmillerstrasse, on the west side of Leopoldstrasse, was home to several turn-of-the-century painters and writers. Both Ainmillerstrasse and Hohenzollernstrasse (Schwabing's foremost shopping street with its boutiques and arcades) are fronted by some magnificent *Jugendstil* facades.

Englischer Garten

From Schwabing, head east to the lovely **Englischer Garten** ㉒. Opened in 1793, the park was the brainchild of an American-born adventurer who had sided with the British in the American Revolution. Better known to the Bavarians as Count Rumford, Benjamin Thompson drew his inspiration from the English landscape gardeners Capability Brown and William Chambers. In fact, the **Chinesischer Turm** (Chinese Tower), a decorative pagoda that moonlights as a bandstand in the popular beer garden, owes a great deal to Chambers' Cantonese Pagoda in London's Kew Gardens. The natural landscaping is still a joy for visitors, including, famously, the nudists who stretch out along the Eisbach stream in

The Maximilianeum

the southern part of the park. The **Monopteros** (love temple) atop a grassy mound south of the Chinese Tower is an attractive focal point from which to admire the city's skyline.

The gardens stretch almost 5km (3 miles) to the north. Stroll up to the **Kleinhesseloher See**, a boating pond with a café and beer garden on its eastern side; beyond, in the northern part of the park, you can walk beside the River Isar. In the southwest corner, the pretty **Japanese Tea House** was donated by Japan to commemorate the 1972 Olympic Games. Just beyond the Tea House, at Prinzregentenstrasse 1, the **Haus der Kunst** (House of Art; www.hausderkunst.de; charge) is a venue for temporary exhibitions and theatre. Originally called the Haus der Deutschen Kunst, this

Boats lining the Kleinhesseloher

DEGENERATE ART

Hitler's speech inaugurating the Haus der Deutschen Kunst in 1937 attacked the 'obscenities' of avant-garde art and forbade any painter to use colours that the 'normal' eye could not perceive in nature. Two exhibitions were held to distinguish so-called great German art from that designated 'degenerate art'.

The trouble was that the 'degenerate' show was far more popular, and attracted two million visitors, five times as many as the other exhibition. Afterwards, many of these paintings, including works by Kandinsky, Mondrian, Kokoschka, and Chagall, were hidden away or sold abroad for valuable foreign currency. Today, some of these works are on display again in the Pinakothek der Moderne.

is another building from the Nazi era. Built as a temple to Hitler's personal vision of a truly German art, the monotonous construction was soon nicknamed the 'Palazzo Kitschi' by Munich wits.

Prinzregentenstrasse

Further out along Prinzregentenstrasse is the **Bayerisches Nationalmuseum** ㉓ (www.bayerisches-nationalmuseum.de; charge). Built in 1900, the exterior mirrors the artistic evolution of the periods exhibited inside – a Romanesque east wing, a later Renaissance western facade, a Baroque tower and, finally, a Rococo west wing. The collection spans German cultural history from the Middle Ages to the nineteenth century, emphasising both religious and secular arts and craftsmanship. One of the highlights is a collection of wooden sculptures by the Late Gothic master Tilman Riemenschneider.

Now walk across Prinzregentenbrücke, crossing the river to the **Friedensengel** (Angel of Peace), high on her pillar. Begun in 1896, the monument celebrates the 25 years of peace that followed the German defeat of the French in 1871. Portraits of the architects

NOTES

The 2021-opened Gasteig HP8 cultural centre, at the edge of the Sendling district, is the younger sibling of the temporarily closed Kulturzentrum am Gasteig, which has been at the forefront of the arts scene for forty years. The new arts hub is home to a variety of theatres, the Münchner Stadtbibliothek library and the Isarphilharmonie concert hall. It will serve as the temporary host of events and exhibitions multiyear renovations are ongoing at the original, slated for completion in 2027 (www.fatcat-muc.de).

of that period – Bismarck, Kaisers Wilhelm I and II, and the generals Moltke and von der Tann – decorate the facade. The mosaics of *Peace*, *War*, *Victory* and the *Blessings of Culture* indicate the rather ambiguous nature of the celebration.

There's nothing ambiguous, however, about the **Villa Stuck**, at Prinzregentenstrasse 60, which was built in 1898 for the last in Munich's line of painter-princes, Franz von Stuck. He amassed a fortune rivalling that of Franz von Lenbach by combining the new artistic trends of *Jugendstil* symbolism with the prevailing salon taste. His opulent villa is the perfect setting for the **Jugendstil Museum** (www.villastuck.de; charge). All the interior decoration and furniture date from the turn of the twentieth century and the house is often used as a venue for temporary exhibitions.

Along the Isar

Highlights

- **Deutsches Museum**, see page 76

South of the Friedensengel, the banks of the River Isar make for a pleasant stroll. Paths wind their way through parkland and along boardwalks just above the water. Above the

Maximiliansbrücke looms the imposing neo-Romanesque facade of the **Maximilianeum**. Completed in 1874, the building was first the home of the Maximilianeum Foundation for Gifted Bavarian Students before becoming seat of the Bavarian Parliament in 1949. At the other side of the bridge, elegant **Maximilianstrasse** leads towards the city centre. The street is named after its creator, Maximilian II (1848–64), who had it lined with buildings designed in a unique Gothic-Renaissance style known as the 'Maximilian style'. Notable structures include the **Museum Fünf Kontinente** (Five Continents Museum; www.museum-fuenf-kontinente.de; charge) and the **Upper Bavarian Government** building opposite; closer into town, at the other side of the inner ring road, is

Among the planes at the Deutsches Museum is a Ju 52

the renowned **Hotel Vier Jahreszeiten**; at this point, before Max-Josef-Platz, Maximilianstrasse becomes Munich's most elegant shopping street.

East of the Maximilianeum is the district of **Haidhausen**. At one time this was an impoverished working-class area, but it now rivals Schwabing as Munich's trendiest quarter, with pleasant streets and plenty of good eateries and nightspots.

Deutsches Museum

The path along the Isar passes the **Müller'sches Volksbad**, the oldest public baths in Munich, completed in 1901. With its opulent *Jugendstil* decor, it's a fine place for a swim and sauna.

Müller'sches Volksbad, the oldest public baths in Munich

To the south, across the bridge and occupying its own river island, the **Deutsches Museum** ㉔ (www.deutsches-museum.de; charge) sprawls across an exhibition area of over 5 hectares (12.5 acres) – Europe's largest museum of science and technology. It was established by the engineer Oskar von Miller in 1903, and opened on its present, purpose-built site in 1925. From the outset, the intention was to entertain as well as educate, so the museum is not just a series of static displays, but also interactive models, experimental machines and audio-visual effects.

It would take days, if not weeks, to see everything in the museum, which is divided into sections for the various classical fields of technology such as mining, road and bridge building, metallurgy and marine navigation, as well as forms of overland transport – from the carriage to the car. Here you can see the world's first automobile – the Benz Welding three-wheeler. Train enthusiasts will love the inaugural German *Lokomobil*, built in 1862 and still operating. British visitors may note with interest that the Germans have on display a replica of *Puffing Billy*, one of the earliest English locomotives, dating from 1813. The power machinery section is also very popular, with its collection of impressive engines and turbines. The marine navigation department covers everything from the earliest dug-out canoes to developments in modern shipbuilding; the highlight is the nineteenth-century fishing boat *Maria,* exhibited alongside an Arab *dhow.*

The first floor is dominated by the department of aeronautics: ordinary balloons, helicopters and jet planes are exhibited beside big-hitters such as Lilienthal's original glider and the legendary Junkers Ju 52, plus an A4 rocket that forms a link with the department of astronautics. On this floor also, the departments of physics and chemistry provide plenty of interactive materials, along with historical artefacts such as the telescope used to discover Neptune. Also worth a look are the musical instruments and automata exhibition and, on the second floor, an exact replica of the prehistoric paintings of the Altamira Cave in Spain.

NOTES

Much space in the Deutsches Museum is devoted to electricity, perhaps because Oskar von Miller himself made important contributions to electrical engineering. One of the main attractions is the thrice-daily demonstration of a high-voltage apparatus which simulates a stroke of lightning.

Outside the city centre

Highlights

- **Schloss Nymphenburg**, see below
- **Olympiapark**, see page 82

Schloss Nymphenburg

Away from the heat of the Residenz in the city centre, **Schloss Nymphenburg** (www.schloss-nymphenburg.de; charge; tram 17) was the Wittelsbachs' summer refuge. The gleaming palace is set in extensive grounds with fountains, ponds and four garden pavilions.

Steinerner Saal ceiling

Together with the Theatinerkirche (see page 58), it was built to celebrate the birth of a new son and heir, Maximilian Emanuel, to Princess Henriette Adelaide in 1662. The palace had modest beginnings as a small summer villa, but it grew over the next century as each succeeding ruler added another wing or pavilion.

The palace is approached by a long canal with avenues on either bank leading to a semicircle of lawns, the Schlossrondell, which is the site of the Royal Porcelain Factory (see page 106). In the central edifice of the

Schloss Nymphenburg

palace proper are galleries of fine eighteenth-century stucco work and ceiling frescoes. The majestic two-storey banquet hall, **Steinerner Saal** (Stone Hall), contains some impressive frescoes by Johann Baptist Zimmermann on the theme *Nymphen huldigen der Göttin Flora* (Nymphs Pay Homage to the Goddess Flora).

To the south, the first pavilion is the home of the famous **Schönheitsgalerie** (Gallery of Beautiful Women). Ludwig I commissioned Joseph Stieler to paint these portraits of Munich's most beautiful young women, including Ludwig's mistress, the dancer Lola Montez.

The **Marstallmuseum**, a dazzling collection of state coaches, has been installed in the south wing, in what was once the royal stables. Starting from the extravagance of Karl Albrecht's eighteenth-century coronation coaches, the vehicles went on to

An autumnal Königssee, near Berchtesgaden

achieve a state of ornamental delirium under Ludwig II. Look for his Nymphenschlitten (Nymph sleigh), designed for escapades in the Alps. On the first floor, the beautiful **Bäuml** collection of Nymphenburg porcelain covers examples of the entire output from the Nymphenburg factory, from the eighteenth century to the 1920s.

Also in the Nymphenburg palace, the extensive **Museum Mensch und Natur** (Man and Nature Museum; www.mmn-muenchen.de; charge) covers the history of the planet and life on earth. The position of humans in the universe and their responsibilities towards the environment are important themes, and numerous ecological topics are explored, such as population growth and hunger.

The gardens were originally laid out in a subdued Italian style for Henriette Adelaide but later lost some of their formality. Off to the left lies the **Amalienburg**, built between 1734 and 1739 by François de Cuvilliés, with the help of sculptor Joachim Dietrich and stucco artist Johann Baptist Zimmermann. Wander round the rooms where the hunting dogs and rifles were kept, the Pheasant Room next to the blue-and-white Dutch-tiled kitchen, and the brilliant silver and pastel-yellow Rococo **Spiegelsaal** (Hall of Mirrors), originally the pavilion's entrance.

Continue west to find the **Badenburg** (Bath Pavilion), fitted with fine Delft china fixtures. The **Grosser See** is a large pond dotted with islands, overlooked by a love temple modelled after Rome's Temple of Vesta, goddess of fire.

North of the central canal, with its spectacular cascade of water, is another, smaller pond. On its far side stands the **Pagodenburg**, an octagonal tea pavilion. The fourth of the park's pavilions is the **Magdalenenklause** (Hermitage), built for Maximilian Emanuel in 1725. Don't be surprised that the building is a crumbling

THE BAVARIAN ALPS

On a clear day, particularly during *Föhn*, the Alps provide a stunning backdrop to the Bavarian countryside and are a playground for hikers and climbers, skiers, paragliders and even sailors and windsurfers. Though lower than some of the mountains in neighbouring Austria, they are nonetheless impressive, with steep limestone ridges running from west to east. In the west they begin with the lower **Allgäu Alps**, where Neuschwanstein is located, but these soon give way to the highest section, the Wetterstein range, which culminates in Germany's highest peak, the **Zugspitze**. Its 2962m/9718ft summit can be reached from **Garmisch**. A break in the mountains is occupied by the picturesque town of **Mittenwald**, above which rise the impressive **Karwendel Mountains** (mostly in Austria). Further to the east, just beyond Chiemsee, the most spectacular scenery of all can be found around **Berchtesgaden** with the east face of the mighty Watzmann (2713m/ 8901ft).

The extraordinary, white-turreted Neuschwanstein Castle

ruin; the cracks and flaking plaster were deliberately incorporated into the mock Romanesque and Gothic structure, and an ornate Moorish minaret was thrown in too.

Olympiapark

In the north of the city, best accessed via the U-Bahn (U3 from Marienplatz), the sport and recreation area of the **Olympiapark** (Olympic Park; www.olympiapark.de) was created for the 1972 Olympic Games.

The complex is dominated by the 291m (954ft) -high **Olympiaturm**, a symbol of the games. The restaurant and observation decks, reopened after renovations in mid-2026, provide spectacular views of the city and surroundings, and on a clear day the Alps can appear almost close enough to touch. The other major feature of the huge complex is the **Olympiastadion**, with its 78,000 seating capacity and extraordinary tent-roof structure. This used to be the home of Bayern Munich.

Nearby stands the distinctive main headquarters of BMW. The bowl-shaped **BMW Museum** (www.bmw-welt.com) provides a fascinating insight into the history of the Bavarian Motor Works, with exhibits of cars, motorcycles and aircraft engines. The futuristic **BMW Welt** showroom complex is another worthwhile attraction to visit.

Into Bavaria

Highlights

- **Neuschwanstein**, see page 84
- **Oberammergau**, see page 86
- **Linderhof**, see page 86
- **The lakes**, see page 87
- **Berchtesgaden**, see page 89
- **The Romantic Road**, see page 92
- **Augsburg**, see page 96
- **Regensburg and around**, see page 97
- **Nuremberg**, see page 98

The Bavarian countryside is at its most beautiful to the south of the city. This is where the plane of southern Bavaria slams into the high Alps, a landscape of dramatic peaks, picturesque lakes, onion-domed churches, tradition-steeped villages and Ludwig II's nineteenth-century castle follies. Another attractive aspect of the region is that it's easily accessible by public transport, with the S-Bahn and regional trains servicing most major attractions.

To the east and northeast of Munich, the Romantic Road (Romantisches Strasse) is a 350km-long tourist route between Würzburg in the north and Füssen in the south, taking in some of Germany's most idyllic medieval walled towns and blockbuster sights along the

NOTES

Fröttmaning, in the north of the city, is home to the 66,000-seat Allianz Arena, built for the 2006 World Cup and as the new home ground for the city's two football teams, FC Bayern München and TSV 1860 München. Its futuristic design enables it to change colour according to which team is playing. It can be reached by the U6 from Marienplatz.

way. Most points on the route are accessible by public transport from Munich, though you may need a car to visit the more obscure locations.

Also to the east (and a stop on the Romantic Road) is Augsburg, a fascinating medieval town that once rivalled Munich in wealth and importance. Further afield, the varied cities of Nuremberg and Regensburg make for intriguing trips into Bavaria's northern and eastern reaches.

Neuschwanstein

Bavaria's (and arguably Germany's) most famous attraction, Neuschwanstein Castle is just over two hours by train or car southwest of Munich. En route, drivers can visit **Landsberg am Lech**, with its interesting medieval town centre, and then take the B17, the Deutsche Alpenstrasse (German Alpine Road). Stop off at Steingaden to visit the lovely **St Johann Baptist Church**, which retains much of its twelfth-century Romanesque exterior. You'll also enjoy the pleasant walk in the old cloister. From Steingaden, it's worth making a detour to visit the magnificent **Wieskirche** ㉕ (www.wieskirche.de), a pilgrimage church dating from 1754 and designed by Dominikus Zimmermann. The ceiling is splashed with a sublime fresco by his brother Johann Baptist, which depicts Christ dispensing divine mercy. In its architecture and decoration, the church is a consummate work – perfect to the last Rococo detail and well deserving of its UNESCO World Cultural Heritage status.

Neuschwanstein Castle ㉖ lies just east of Füssen (www.neuschwanstein.de; charge). A visit in 1867 to the medieval castle of Wartburg in Thuringia first

NOTES

Tickets for both Neuschwanstein and Hohenschwangau can be purchased online at www.hohenschwangau.de, with any remaining tickets for the day sold at the Ticket-Center in Hohenschwangau.

fired Ludwig's imagination with a vision of the Minnesänger, the minstrels of the twelfth century, and he decided to build a castle that would recapture the aura of that romantic era. Ludwig replaced a ruined mountain retreat of his father's in the Schwangau with an extraordinary white-turreted castle. Set in the midst of a forest of fir and pine, it overlooks the gorge of Pöllat and Lake Forggen. Tours include the magnificent throne room, and you can try to imagine, as did Ludwig, the minstrel contests of another age in the Sängersaal. Ludwig II was Wagner's biggest patron, and fans of the composer's works will recognise the sculptural and painted allusions to *Tannhäuser, Die Meistersinger von Nürnberg* and *Tristan und Isolde*.

Neuschwanstein Castle

While Neuschwanstein Castle was being built (it was never completed as Ludwig died when it was only half-finished), Ludwig kept an eye on its progress from the neighbouring castle of **Hohenschwangau**, just 1km (0.5 miles) away. This neo-Gothic building had been constructed by his father, Maximilian II. In fact, Neuschwanstein and Hohenschwangau collectively are known as 'die Königsschlösser'. Take a look at the music room, with its display of Wagner memorabilia (the composer stayed at Hohenschwangau), and Ludwig's bedroom, noted for its star-studded ceiling.

The third attraction here is the impressive **Museum der Bayerischen Könige** (Museum of the Bavarian Kings; www.

The sublime Hohenschwangau

hohenschwangau.de), housed in a former hotel on the shores of the scenic Alpsee lake, a short walk from the Neuschwanstein/ Hohenschwangau ticket office. The interior, filled with refracted light from the lake, tells the story of the Wittelsbachs' 700-year tenancy of the Bavarian throne, though due to the museum's location the focus is naturally on Maximilian II and his son, Ludwig II.

If you want to reach the castles from Munich by public transport, take an early train from the Hauptbahnhof to Füssen, then change to local bus or taxi for the short ride out of town.

Oberammergau and Linderhof

The second of Ludwig's dream castles is reached via **Ettal**, which features a lovely Benedictine monastery set in a gently curving valley. Stop and admire Johann Jakob Zeiller's eighteenth-century fresco of the life of St Benedict. Continue to **Oberammergau** ㉗, setting for the world-famous ten-yearly Passion Play, inaugurated in the plague year of 1633 and still performed by local people. The Passion Play Theatre, where the epic is staged, can be visited on guided tours. In the town are some very well-preserved eighteenth-century facades, adorned with paintings by the so-called *Lüftlmaler* (air painter), Franz Zwinck.

A short ride (or pleasant 12km/7.5 mile hike) west of Oberammergau, Ludwig's favourite castle, remote little **Linderhof** (www.schlosslinderhof.de; charge), was the embodiment of his Baroque fantasies. The palace, inspired by Versailles, is opulent inside and out. Quite apart from the carefully tailored landscape of pond and park, you could be excused for thinking that the whole romantic Alpine backdrop had been created from Ludwig's imagination. Only the Venus Grotto, carved out of the mountainside and forming another Wagnerian motif from *Tannhäuser*, is in fact man-made.

Oberammergau is just under two hours by train from Munich Hauptbahnhof, with a change in Murnau. Regular buses link Oberammergau with Linderhof and Ettal.

The lakes

Ammersee 28 (35km/56 miles southwest of Munich on the A96) is a delightful place for long, serene walks along the lake or up into the tranquil wooded hills. Make a beeline for the Benedictine Abbey of **Andechs** (www.andechs.de), which overlooks Ammersee from the east. The fifteenth-century church was redecorated in the Rococo style by Johann Baptist Zimmermann.

The monks still brew first-rate beer (Andechser) here and the monastery runs a very popular beer hall and

Oberammergau

Dawn breaks over Chiemsee

garden. To reach Ammersee, take the S8 to Herrsching; the trip takes fifty minutes.

The **Starnberger** ㉙, the northern tip of which is just 22km from Munich city centre, is one of the most popular day-trips for city dwellers looking to escape the stifling urban heat. The town of **Starnberg** on the northern shore is just a jumping-off point for the lake measuring 20km (12 miles) from north to south. Relax in the area's quiet, rural scenery and wander along the peaceful rush-fringed shoreline or hike the five kilometres along the lake edge to Schloss Berg on the eastern side, where in 1886 Ludwig II was found drowned with his doctor in just a few feet of water. It remains a mystery how this came to pass; a dramatic cross rises out of the water to mark the spot. Starnberg can be reached by train in twenty minutes.

Chiemsee ㉚ (70km/43 miles southeast of Munich) is the largest lake in Bavaria and the location of Ludwig II's most ambitious castle. **Herrenchiemsee** (www.herrenchiemsee.de; charge) is situated on an island, the Herreninsel, at the western end of the lake and reached by ferry. Ludwig started work on it in 1878, but ran out of money and time, in 1886. Nevertheless, he made a valiant attempt at recreating the grandeur of Versailles, and the magnificent **Spiegelsaal** (Hall of Mirrors) can certainly bear comparison with the Galerie des Glaces. The building, few can fail to notice, pays ample homage to the king Ludwig admired most, Louis XIV. On a tiny island nearby is **Frauenchiemsee**, where Duke Tassilo III founded a Benedictine convent in 782. As well as the former convent there are some charming little fishing cottages and restaurants.

Using trains from the Hauptbahnhof, head to Prien (one hour) from where ferries to the Herreninsel depart.

Berchtesgaden

Once a favourite summer retreat of the Bavarian royal family, the delightful small town of **Berchtesgaden** and its surroundings encapsulate all the attractions of the Bavarian Alps. Painted houses, a small royal palace and fine views contribute to the allure of the town, which is also the home of the **Nationalparkhaus** (www.nationalpark-berchtesgaden.de), the interpretive centre for the national park that protects the area's sublime but vulnerable landscape. The town's ancient prosperity depended on salt, and visitors can enjoy a thrilling trip into the depths of the old salt mines, the **Salzbergwerk** (www.salzzeitreise.de; charge). Another trip is up the mountain road to the **Kehlsteinhaus**, also known as the 'Eagle's Nest', Hitler's perch atop the 1834m (6017ft) Kehlstein, now a panoramic restaurant. Near the foot of the mountain is the **Dokumentation Obersalzberg** (www.obersalzberg.de), an information centre documenting the area's Third Reich connections. But the essential excursion in this region is aboard one of the eco-friendly electric boats that cruise

The Baroque facade of Schloss Schleissheim

the crystal-clear turquoise waters of the **Königssee** ㉛, affording views of Germany's second-highest peak, the Watzmann (2713m/8900ft), and tying up along the much-photographed onion-domed church of **St Bartholomä**. From here walking trails lead into some dramatic mountainscape; the best walk is a 6km/4 mile easy-going there-back hike to the **Eiskapelle**, a huge ice cavern.

With your own wheels, Berchtesgaden is an easy day trip from Munich along the A8 motorway (and an even easier one from Salzburg just across the border with Austria). By train from Munich's Hauptbahnhof the trip takes just three hours, with a change in Freilassing.

North of Munich

Dachau (17km/11 miles northwest of Munich) used to be known primarily for the remains of a sixteenth-century château and its fine eighteenth-century facades. Then, on 20 March 1933, after Hitler had been in power for a mere 48 days, Dachau was designated as the site of the first Nazi concentration camp. Today, while you can still appreciate the charming town centre, the main dark tourism attraction is the **Dachau Concentration Camp Memorial Site** ㉜ (www.kz-gedenkstaette-dachau.de), which occupies the former camp. Exhibitions document the camp's sinister history in a moving and often disturbing way (it's not recommended children visit the museum). Dachau was not an extermination camp but served as a detention centre for political prisoners; even so, 31,951 deaths were recorded between 1933 and 1945. You can see the original crematorium and gas chambers (labelled 'Bad' for showers), built but never used, as well as reconstructed prison barracks.

To reach the concentration camp, take the S2 to Dachau then change onto regular city bus 726, alighting at the KZ-Gedenkstätte bus stop.

Schloss Schleissheim (www.schloesser-schleissheim.de; charge) in Munich's northern suburbs is another worthwhile half-day trip from the city centre. The Neues Schloss has a glorious staircase with frescoes by Cosmas Damian Asam. Beautiful stucco work adorns banqueting halls and galleries such as the Barockgalerie, containing a fine collection of seventeenth-century Dutch and Flemish paintings. The gardens, complete with waterfall and canals, are a triumph of French landscape design. Be sure to visit the **Schloss Lustheim** hunting lodge at the eastern end. Nearby, a branch of the Deutsches Museum, the **Flugwerft Schleissheim** (www.deutsches-museum.de/en/flugwerft/information; charge) houses an impressive collection of flying machines, a must for children and potential pilots.

The castles and the museum are around fifteen minutes' walk from Oberschleissheim S-Bahn station on the S1 line.

Freising is the closest town to Munich Airport, and could fill half a day while waiting for a flight (regular buses run to and from the terminals). Once the seat of the local bishop, the main attraction here is the huge hilltop cathedral dedicated to Sts Maria and Korbinian, the interior of which is another masterly Baroque collaboration by the Asam brothers. For some less sober pleasures, head to the **Weihenstephan Monastery** (www.weihenstephaner.de), said to be the oldest brewery in the world. Tours end with a tasting session.

Freising station is reached by train in around 25 minutes, or in fifty minutes by S-Bahn.

The Romantic Road

Stretching for 350km from the vineyards of Würzburg to the foothills of the Alps at Füssen, the **Romantic Road** (Romantische Strasse) is Germany's most popular tourist route. You could spend a month exploring this string of medieval walled towns, hilltop castles, mighty cathedrals and pretty churches, and all but the most remote of the sights are just a short train ride (or two) from Munich Hauptbahnhof. The stopping-off points form some of the most enchanting outings from the Bavarian capital.

Würzburg 33 marks the start of the Romantic Road's journey south. This city on the River Main was once the seat of the Prince-Bishops, one of whom, Schönborn, enjoyed a lavish lifestyle in the magnificent UNESCO-listed **Residenz** (www.residenz-wuerzburg.de; charge) built for him by the famous central European architect, Balthasar Neumann. This is one of the largest and most flamboyant Baroque palaces in Germany, boasting a succession of opulent interiors and, crowning the huge staircase, the largest ceiling painting in the world, the work of the Venetian artist Tiepolo. At the centre of the Franconian vineyards, Würzburg has a relaxed atmosphere. There's a winery in the late-medieval hospice known

Rothenburg ob der Tauber in the Old Town

as the Juliusspital, and a tour of the wine-producing villages along the Main is highly recommended, as is a visit to the Prince-Bishops' Baroque summer palace at **Veitshöchheim** (www.schloesser.bayern.de; charge), 7km (4 miles) from Würzburg. This is the country's most famous Rococo garden, studded with more than two hundred statues.

NOTES

Rothenburg was spared from destruction in the Thirty Years' War when its mayor successfully downed a 3.25 litre (nearly 6 pint) draught of wine in one gulp, a seemingly impossible feat, recreated each year at the Meistertrunk Festival in late May.

Würzburg is 280km from Munich. The train journey takes just two hours.

Rothenburg ob der Tauber ㉞ is an essential stop along the way, its quaint name matching the city's seventeenth-century looks, reconstructed after significant wartime destruction. Blank out the crowds of visitors wandering the streets, relax in the main square, or file along the sentry-walk running the whole length of the 2.5km (1.5 mile) fortifications to be transported magically back into an idealised Bavaria of the Middle Ages. There's an excellent view from the tall tower of the Renaissance Rathaus over Rothenburg's red-tiled rooftops to the serene Franconian countryside. A stroll around the streets reveals an almost-endless succession of delightful townscapes, none more photographed than the **Plönlein**, a cobbled space of changing levels framed by towers and half-timbered houses.

Rothenburg ob der Tauber is a feasible day trip from Munich by car, but the train journey requires two changes (either at Treuchtlingen and Steinach, or Nuremberg and Ansbach) and takes 2hr 30min to 3hr 30min.

Dinkelsbühl ㉟ is another picturesque town, with intact defences, pastel-hued townhouses, a fine parish church and slightly fewer visitors. It also escaped obliteration during the Thirty Years' War when its children appealed en masse to a besieging general. The event is recreated at the annual Kinderzeche festival. A day-trip to Dinkelsbühl is only possible if you have your own car.

Nördlingen, is also a well-preserved medieval town sporting intact ramparts interspersed with sixteen towers and five gateways, but has a slightly more workaday feel and far fewer visitors than Rothenburg. The top sight here is the unique **Rieskrater Museum** (www.rieskrater-museum.de), devoted to explaining the story of the 25km (16 mile) diameter crater, formed by a giant meteorite fifteen million years ago, at the centre of which the town lies. A treat for steam train buffs is the **Bayerisches Eisenbahnmuseum**

The dramatic Burg Harburg

(Bavarian Railway Museum; www.bayerisches-eisenbahnmuseum.de; charge), displaying various German locos from down the ages. Summer steam specials run north to Dombühl (via Dinkelsbühl) and Gunzenhausen.

Medieval Nördlingen

Nördlingen can be reached by train in 2hr 30min from Munich's Hauptbahnhof with a change in Donauwörth.

Burg Harburg 36 (www.burg-harburg.de) is arguably the Romantic Road's most dramatic castle, peeking out from a wooded hilltop with views of the tranquil countryside for miles around. The eleventh-century stronghold was remodelled in the eighteenth century and the interior holds collections of tapestry, gold and silver.

Harburg is two hours by train from Munich with a change in Donauwörth, ten minutes away. A visit is best combined with half a day in Donauwörth.

Donauwörth may not be the most popular stop-off on the Romantic Road, but this attractive town at the confluence of the Danube and Wörnitz river is definitely worth half a day's perusal. The thirteenth-century **Rathaus** (town hall) has a carillon that puts on daily performances at 11am and 4pm. At the other end of Reichstrasse, the main thoroughfare, the fifteenth-century **Liebfraukirche** has an unusual sloping floor and a climbable tower affording views as far as the Alps.

Augsburg, founded in 15 BC, was named after Emperor Augustus

Donauwörth is simple to reach by rail, with trains making the journey direct from Munich in fifty minutes.

South of Donauwörth the next stop on the Romantic Road is Augsburg. About 90km/56 miles south of Augsburg is the Baroque Wieskirche (see page 84). The Romantic Road comes to a fitting climax at the gates of Neuschwanstein Castle (see page 84).

Augsburg

Founded in 15 BC and named after Emperor Augustus, **Augsburg**, 50km (31 miles) from Munich, had its heyday in the late Middle Ages, when the Fugger family made it Central Europe's banking centre. Their **Fuggerei** (www.fugger.de; charge), a gated complex of old people's homes, was the first of its kind in the world, and is still home to deserving pensioners. With streets and squares beautified by Renaissance fountains and lined with fine townhouses, Augsburg is a stately city, its pride and wealth on ostentatious display in the Golden Hall of the **Rathaus** and in the sumptuous furnishings and fittings of the cathedral. Augsburg is 35 minutes by rail from Munich's main station.

Regensburg and around

Regensburg ㊲, 130km (81 miles) north of Munich, has many historical delights. Founded by the Romans to guard their frontier on the Danube, in the Middle Ages it was the biggest city in Bavaria, and has kept a wealth of ancient buildings lining the grid pattern of streets and alleyways established by the Romans. Unique in Germany are the fortified towerhouses built by prosperous medieval merchant families to flaunt their wealth and status; some thirty of these extraordinary structures have survived. Another remarkable survivor is the **Steinerne Brücke** (Stone Bridge), a fifteen-span marvel of medieval engineering thrown across the Danube in the mid-twelfth century.

From the bridge there is a fine prospect of the city still looking much as it must have done in the Middle Ages; beyond the gateway and clock tower guarding the bridge approach

Regensburg

rises Regensburg's **Dom** (Cathedral), the finest Gothic structure in Bavaria, begun in the thirteenth century and completed in the nineteenth with the addition of delicate openwork spires. Its sculpture of the 'Laughing Angel' is famous, as is its array of stained glass. The city's most illustrious family was the princely dynasty of Thurn and Taxis, pioneers in the sixteenth century of a reliable postal service. The opulent lifestyle they enjoyed is on show in the **Schloss St Emmeram** (www.thurnundtaxis.de). The guided tour also takes in lovely medieval cloisters.

High above the Danube a short distance downstream from Regensburg stands the gleaming white neo-Grecian temple of **Walhalla** (www.schloesser.bayern.de), built by King Ludwig I of Bavaria in 1842 to honour Germany's heroes. Its array of more than 120 busts begins with the tenth-century King Henry the Fowler, and it is still being added to; the latest to be honoured is Sophie Scholl, the Munich student executed by the Nazis for her resistance to the regime.

Half-timbered architecture of the Old Town, Nuremberg

Regensburg is 1hr 30min by train from Munich and less than two hours up the A9 and A93 by car.

Nuremberg

Rebuilt after wartime devastation, the Altstadt in Nürnberg (Nuremberg)

Salzstadel in Regensburg

conveys the atmosphere of the archetypal German medieval city, with formidable defensive walls, streets lined with red-roofed old buildings, squares presided over by great Gothic churches and fabulous fountains. Overlooking it all from a rocky summit is an Imperial castle.

The unchallenged capital of northern Bavaria, **Nuremberg** 38 is associated not just with emperors and Wagner's Mastersingers, but also with some of the grimmer aspects of Nazism, in particular the ostentatious pageantry of party rallies and the postwar trials of the Third Reich's leaders.

The Altstadt is split into roughly equal halves by the River Pegnitz, which is spanned by the picturesque **Heilig-Geist-Spital**, a fifteenth-century almshouse. To the south, the twin-towered **Lorenzkirche** (Church of St Lawrence) contains masterworks by

The Germanisches Nationalmuseum shelters a huge collection of artefacts

the great craftsmen the city nurtured at its zenith in the fifteenth and early sixteenth centuries, as does the lovely **Frauenkirche** (Church of Our Lady) to the north.

The Frauenkirche has a glockenspiel with performing automata, while the marketplace it occupies is the festive scene of the Christkindlmarkt, Nuremberg's world-famous Christmas market. Here, too, is the 19m (62ft) Gothic **Schöner Brunnen**, the city's foremost fountain, studded with an astonishing array of ornate statuary.

From here, Burgstrasse leads upwards past the Sebaldskirche and Rathaus to the **Kaiserburg** (Imperial Castle; www.kaiserburg-nuernberg.de), a complex structure begun in the twelfth century by Emperor Frederick Barbarossa. From the main tower there is a fine panorama over the Altstadt. Below the castle is the **Albrecht Dürer Haus** (www.museen.nuernberg.de/duererhaus), the residence of Nuremberg's most famous son.

Some of the artist's finest work can be seen in the enormous **Germanisches Nationalmuseum** (www.gnm.de; charge, free Wed evening), whose huge collection of artefacts spans German culture from the earliest time.

Just beyond the city walls, the **DB Museum** (German Railways Museum; www.dbmuseum.de; charge) is the largest of its kind in

Germany, housing a fine collection of railway artefacts and a huge model railway. Southeast of the city centre, some of the monster structures erected for the Nazi Party rallies still stand, notably the incomplete congress centre modelled on Rome's Colosseum.

Part of it now houses the Dokumentationszentrum Reichsparteitagsgelände (https://museen.nuernberg.de/dokuzentrum; charge), a documentation centre chronicling the Third Reich and Nuremberg's role in it.

Trains leave Munich's Hauptbahnhof for Nuremberg regularly, completing the journey in just over an hour. By car it takes around two hours.

Nuremberg's Imperial castle overlooks the red-roofed city from its rocky summit

Cuvilliés-Theater's opulent interior

Things to do

With its mix of contemporary art spaces, world-class museums and rich musical legacy, Germany's third-largest city has a playful spirit and youthful energy. Munich has no problem in providing culture – there's something here to suit every taste.

Music

First and foremost, Munich is a city of music, with four major symphony orchestras: the Bavarian State Orchestra, Munich Philharmonic, Bavarian Radio Symphony and Munich Symphony Orchestra. The main concerts are performed at the **Gasteig HP8**, the temporary home for the big-hitting Kulturzentrum am Gasteig while it undergoes major renovation works until 2027.

In summer there are **open-air concerts** on Odeonsplatz and Königsplatz, or you can enjoy performances in the palatial setting of Nymphenburg, Blutenburg, or Schleissheim. Music does not stop during the winter, when concerts are hosted in the Frauenkirche and many other churches in town.

Opera

Opera has long been a Munich attraction. The town vies with Bayreuth for performances of Wagner, and the works of Mozart and Richard Strauss are firm favourites. The Nationaltheater makes every opera evening seem like a gala. The Bavarian State Orchestra plays under the world's greatest conductors, and the summer festival (*Münchner Opernfestspiele*) in June and July attracts the best international singers.

Jazz

Jazz is a favourite in Munich; internationally acclaimed musicians play nightly in many places, most notably at the Unterfahrt im Einstein (www.unterfahrt.de), Einsteinstrasse 42, and at Mister

A bustling beer tent at the Oktoberfest

B's (www.mister-bs.bar), Herzog-Heinrich-Strasse 38, both in Haidhausen. In summer you can also find jazz and dixie musicians playing daily at the Waldwirtschaft beer garden (www.waldwirtschaft.de).

Rock, pop and alternative music

Munich is a major venue for **rock and pop concerts**, attracting a steady stream of international acts. The biggest bands play in the Olympic Stadium; other venues include the Olympiahalle, the Muffathalle, Schlachthof, Elserhalle and Backstage. The **Tollwood Festival**, Munich's lively outdoor music, theatre and art event, held in the southern part of the Olympia Park in June and July, stages well-known global bands and World Music artists to its concert tents.

The quirky **Bahnwärter Thiel** complex (www.bahnwaerterthiel.de) in Schlachthofviertel, south of the centre, puts on alternative music events year-round, with open-air concerts announced on its social media feeds.

Nightlife

The area around Münchener Freiheit in Schwabing is the best-known nightlife district; **Feilitzstrasse** and **Occamstrasse** are peppered with clubs and pubs. Haidhausen is Munich's other cool hangout spot. The **Glockenbachviertel**, located south of Sendlinger Tor, is the focus of the LGBTQ+ scene, and nearby, on the streets radiating from Gärtnerplatz, a large number of hip new bars have opened up. For nightclubs head behind the **Ostbahnhof** (Friedenstrasse), where the Kultfabrik (www.werksviertel-mitte.de) houses 29 clubs, bars and eateries, and Optimolwerke (www.optimolwerke.de) hosts a further eight nightspots.

To find out what's happening when you're in Munich, get hold of a copy of the monthly programme from the Tourist Office or visit www.munich-tourist.de.

Shopping

Munich is an elegant town, the capital of Germany's fashion industry, so there's no lack of upmarket boutiques, especially on **Theatinerstrasse**, **Maximilianstrasse** and on Schwabing's **Leopoldstrasse**. The **Fünf Höfe** (Five Courtyards) shopping precinct between Theatinerstrasse and Kardinal-Faulhaber-Strasse is another coveted address.

What to buy

Munich is also the place for the world's best selection of **tailored garments** (coats, jackets and suits) made in Loden cloth, a Bavarian speciality. This waterproof wool fabric, originally developed for hunters, has kept the people of Munich warm for over a hundred years.

Fünf Höfe (Five Courtyards) shopping precinct

You may even fancy trying on the **Bavarian folk costume** (*Tracht*). There are smart green-collared grey jackets or brightly coloured *Dirndl* dresses with a full gathered skirt and fitted bodice. *Lederhosen*, those slap-happy traditional shorts for Bavarians, are also widely available.

Nymphenburg porcelain is still turned out in traditional Rococo designs. You can peruse pieces (and make a purchase) at the factory in Schloss Nymphenburg (www.nymphenburg.com; see page 78). Pottery connoisseurs should be on the lookout for old **Meissen** or modern **Rosenthal**.

Cutlery, kitchen utensils and electronic gadgets are of a very high standard and superbly designed. You might also like to consider **linens**, in modern or traditional designs, which are renowned for their excellent old-fashioned quality. A great way to save on winter heating bills is to invest in a sumptuous duck or goose-down *Federbett* or eiderdown, another good buy.

The country has always produced excellent children's toys; its industrial prowess is reflected in the intricate building sets and model trains.

The presence of so many great orchestras and musicians in Germany means that the selection of recorded music here is probably second only to the United States. The production of instruments, such as the finest grand pianos, violins and even harmonicas, also enjoys a venerable reputation.

Outdoor activities

The city's great boon to sports lovers was the construction of the Olympic facilities in 1972. All year round, ice-skating fans gather at the Olympic ice rink. The swimming pool at the Olympia Schwimmhalle (www.olympiapark.de) can be used by anyone, as can around a dozen other indoor and open-air pools (*Freibäder*) dotted around the city. The outdoor pools, which open in May, are a summertime institution in Munich; they are superbly maintained, and all provide lawns for sunbathing. Most of the indoor pools are equipped with saunas and other wellness facilities; the Cosimabad (www.swm.de/baeder/cosimawellenbad) has a wave pool and the award-winning Westbad has a 60m slide, while the Müller'sches Volksbad (www.swm.de/baeder/muellersches-volksbad) is a beautiful *Jugendstil*-era pool. The Dante-Winter-Warmfreibad (www.swm.de/baeder/freibaeder-muenchen/dantebad) has a heated outdoor pool, which is a hit all year, even in snowy winters.

Munich has its share of tennis courts, too: the best are at Olympiapark and in the Englischer Garten.

Jogging and running in the Englischer Garten is fun, especially the stretch along the River Isar. Running in the city is also pleasant, as long as you strike out early to avoid the traffic. For decent exercise combined with lovely scenery, try cycling the 14km (9 miles) along the river path to Ismaning,

NOTES

The 'Auer Dult' is a seasonal flea market dating back to the fourteenth century. It takes place over nine days, three times a year (May, July and October) in the Au district (around Mariahilfplatz, south of the Deutsches Museum). There are invariably some interesting bargains to be found.

or any of the bike routes wiggling throughout Munich. For people who don't want to exert themselves, delightful raft trips (*Flossfahrten*) are organised at weekends.

You can drift slowly down the Isar from Wolfratshausen to Munich, while the beer flows and brass bands play. Book well in advance at www.flossfun.de.

There are fifteen golf courses within a radius of 20km (12 miles) of the city. Courses in the Munich area include Eichenried, Feldafing, Olching, Wörthsee and Margarethenhof am Tegernsee.

Further out of Munich you can sail or windsurf on Ammersee, Starnberger See, Tegernsee and Chiemsee. The local lakes and rivers also offer good fishing.

Olympiapark

Hiking is a major pastime, especially as you approach the Bavarian Alps. Just 97km (61 miles) from Munich, Garmisch-Partenkirchen provides guides for mountain climbing. There are plenty of peaks to tackle, including the 2962m (9717ft) -high Zugspitze. Once you're in the Alps, the whole range of winter sports is at your disposal. Garmisch has, in addition to skiing (and a very professional ski school), its own Olympic rink for skating and ice hockey. The more sedate can try curling, and for the more adventurous there is a bobsled run.

A DAY AT THE ZOO

At the **Hellabrunn Zoo** (U3 U-Bahn or bus No 52 to Thalkirchen from Marienplatz; www.hellabrunn.de), animals are grouped according to their continent of origin, and you'll see zoological curiosities such as the tarpan and the white-tailed gnu. The chimps 'working out' in their own gym is a hit with audiences. It's possible to spend hours in the kids' area alone, with pony rides and goat pens, plus a superb adventure playground and suspension bridge.

Children's Munich

Munich is a wonderful city for children, at any time of year and in any weather. Many of the museums are suitable for kids, but the **Deutsches Museum** (www.deutsches-museum.de; see page 76) is the biggest hit by far, with plenty of fascinating machines and models to play with, and hands-on exhibits for young visitors to operate for themselves. Adults can accompany kids aged 10 or under to the **Kinderreich** section, where they can explore a variety of scientific phenomena such as light, sound and energy through interactive activities. Children can build a house with giant building blocks and play water games in WaterWorld.

The **Museum Mensch und Natur** (www.mmn-muenchen.de; see page 80) is an excellent museum that explores a variety of issues on the subject of humanity, nature and ecology, and is full of weird and wonderful exhibits sure to keep all ages entertained.

You could also try the **Spielzeugmuseum** on Marienplatz (www.spielzeugmuseummuenchen.de), which traces four centuries of toy development. Older children will be delighted by the **Magic Bavaria Erlebnismuseum** (www.magicbavaria.com), an interactive upside-down museum with immersive experiences and the city's largest ball pool, or by the optical illusions at the **WOW Museum** (www.wow-museum.de; see page 49).

Bavaria Filmstadt

Sea Life (www.visitsealife.com) in the Olympiapark introduces children to the underwater environment of rivers and seas, while the **BMW Museum** (www.bmw-welt.com) has displays of cars and motorbikes (see page 82).

Last but by no means least, south of the zoo, at Geiselgasteig, the **Bavaria Filmstadt** (www.filmstadt.de) offers a behind-the-scenes glimpse into the cinema and TV industry and offers 4D cinema experiences.

Festivals

It seems something is always being celebrated in Munich. More than a hundred days a year are officially given over to festivals, processions, banquets and street dances commemorating events such as the arrival of the first strong beer of the year (*Starkbierzeit*) or the departure – often, several centuries ago – of this plague or that occupying army. In fact, any excuse will do.

Running from 7 January, **Fasching** (Carnival) is almost as mad in Munich as it is in the Rhineland. Some 2500 balls are held all over town for police and doctors, lawyers and butchers, artists and plumbers. There are masked processions, and market folk at the Viktualienmarkt have their special dance at midday on Shrove Tuesday.

The biggest blowout of all is the **Oktoberfest**. This began when the Crown Prince Ludwig (later Ludwig I) celebrated his marriage to Princess Theresa in October 1810 with a horse race – and everybody turned up. They came again the next year, too, and the year after, and they've been pouring into the city from around the world ever since.

Although the horse race has been dropped and the festivities now take place during the warmer second half of September, the blushing bride is not forgotten – the name of the site to the west of the city centre on which the Oktoberfest is held is Theresienwiese (though locals refer to it as the *Wies'n*, which is also a nickname for the festival).

The festival begins with a procession of *Wies'n* brewers and innkeepers with their splendidly decorated beer wagons, followed by the one carrying the Festival Queen. For two weeks after the mayor has tapped the first barrel, revellers knock back gargantuan quantities of beer, toted around ten litres at a time by the strong-armed beer maids. This brew washes down huge numbers of barbecued chickens, sausages and spit roasts.

And to work all that off, there's the fun of the fair, with roller-coasters, giant Ferris wheel and dodgem cars.

Calendar of events

For the most up-to-date information on the city's festivals and arts calendar, including a current list of times and dates, ask the tourist information office for its monthly programme of events, or consult the local press.

7 January to Ash Wednesday Fasching: costumed balls and processions.

Mid-March Starkbierzeit: making and sampling of special strong beers during the week including 19 March (St Joseph's Day), always ending in '-ator' like Salvator.

End of April Frühlingsfest (Spring Fair): funfair, concerts. Auer Dult: flea market, over nine days from the last Saturday in April (also in July and Oct).

Mid-June Stadtgründungsfest (Foundation of the City): weekend around 14 June.

June Corpus Christi: colourful street procession from the Frauenkirche to Maxvorstadt; people and horses wear traditional costumes.

End of June Filmfest München (Munich Film Festival, last week of June): at selected cinemas.

June/July Tollwood Sommerfestival: a three-week open-air extravaganza of music, art and theatre from around the world, held in the southern part of the Olympiapark. Nymphenburger Schlosskonzerte: concerts in the palace and grounds of Schloss Nymphenburg.

3 weeks in July Opernfestspiele: a variety of opera performances that take place at the Nationaltheater and Cuvilliés-Theater.

September/October Oktoberfest: sixteen days up to the first Sunday in October. Commemorates the marriage of Ludwig I to Princess Theresa in 1810. Beer drinking, hog roasts, funfair and processions.

December Christkindlmarkt (Christmas market): market offering crafts and gifts for the season on and around Marienplatz. Further markets at Münchner Freiheit, Weissenburger Platz and Rotkreuzplatz, and at the Chinese Tower in the English Garden. Tollwood Winterfestival at Theresienwiese.

Food and drink

Eating and drinking are favourite pastimes in Munich. Conviviality reigns supreme, both in the temples of gastronomy and at the long, communal tables of the *Bräuhaus, Gaststätte, Gasthaus, Wirtschaft* and *Biergarten*.

Besides the fantastic traditional restaurants, Munich's dining scene is rapidly innovating. The city is increasingly embracing global flavours, immersive experiences, regional organic ingredients and sustainability. Skip the *Bräuhaus* (brewhouse) in favour of something special – dining in a repurposed train perhaps, a community café run by refugees or a plant-based menu at a zero-waste kitchen.

Swanky hotel restaurants typically serve Alpine-Adriatic fusion food, while buzzy brunch and wine bars flourish in every district. Munich today offers a rich and often surprising culinary experience for every type of visitor.

A famous Bavarian Bräuhaus

Beer halls and beer gardens

The most popular restaurants for visitors are the *Gaststätte* or *Bräuhaus* – literally meaning 'brewery', but in fact a beer hall. These places usually serve full meals in addition to beer. All the great breweries

The beer garden at the Chinese Tower in the English Garden

have their own beer halls in Munich, and beer gardens, too. You can either bring your own picnic along to the latter or choose from an array of traditional specialities served up at the various food stands.

Weinstuben (traditional taverns), less common in Bavaria than in other regions of Germany, typically serve meals and wine by the glass rather than by the bottle.

In a separate category is the *Konditorei*, a café-pastry shop, the bourgeois fairyland where you can while away a whole afternoon reading the newspapers provided. This is the perfect place for a feast of pastry, ice cream, coffee, tea and fruit juices, with a good choice of wines. Most provide a limited selection of light snacks and salads.

SEASONAL DRINKING

It's not just at the Oktoberfest that the beer flows. In the third and fourth weeks before Easter, the so-called *Starkbierzeit* (Strong-beer time), breweries promote their *Märzenbier* (March ale). After Easter comes the *Maibockzeit*, when they push the strong, dark stuff. In the summer, everybody's thirsty enough not to need too much prompting.

Munich also has several street markets that offer light bites and drinks. The Viktualienmarkt in the city centre and the Elisabethmarkt in Schwabing are well worth a visit.

Top 10 things to try

1. Wurst

When it comes to sausage, the majority of recipes in Munich feature pork, but occasionally beef or veal, flavoured with spices and peppercorns. Pork and veal are combined to create *Weisswürste* (white sausages), spiked with pepper, parsley and onions. *Bratwurst*, another meaty staple on the dining table, is made with

Bavarian sausage served on sauerkraut

just pork and is grilled or sautéed. Another one to try is the spicy *Blutwurst* (blood sausage).

2. Schnitzel

There are at least five types of schnitzel that you can try in Munich. The most common is *Wiener Schnitzel* – a breaded and fried cutlet made of pork rather than veal, served with a slice of lemon and chips. Other popular variations include *Jägerschnitzel* (slathered with mushroom gravy), *Zigeunerschnitzel* (smothered with a spicy pepper and tomato sauce) and *Rahmschnitzel* (topped with a cream sauce).

Paprika schnitzel

3. Leberkäs

During your time in Munich, keep your eyes peeled for *Leberkäs*. Literally translated as 'liver-cheese', this tasty snack in fact contains neither liver nor cheese, but is rather a meatloaf made from pork, bacon and beef, cooked with nutmeg, marjoram and onions. It can be eaten hot or cold.

4. Schweinshaxe

Pork ranks among the most popular meats in many traditional recipes in Germany, including *Schweinshaxe* (roasted knuckle) and *Rippchen* (ribs). Another favourite is the charcoal-grilled *Rostbratwurst* (pork sausage), made in Munich with a recipe dating to 1404.

Schweinshaxe (roasted knuckle)

5. Potato dishes and side salads

Potatoes are a staple ingredient on kitchen tables across Bavaria, with the humble spud making its way into everything from traditional recipes to more modern interpretations. Try *Kartoffelpuffer* (crispy grated-potato pancakes) or *Pellkartoffeln mit Quark und Leinöl*, a combination of boiled potatoes, soft cheese and linseed oil. Other variations include *Bratkartoffeln* (chunky roasted wedges), *Kartoffelbrei* (creamy mash) and *Kartoffelsalat* (potato salad). If you've had your fill of potatoes, other tasty sides include *Gurkensalat*, cucumber and onion marinated in sour cream, vinegar and dill, and *Weisskrautsalat*, a white cabbage salad sometimes referred to as German coleslaw.

6. Bread

German bakers turn out a huge range of products, from breakfast rolls (*Brötchen* or *Semmel*) to sourdough and rye loaves. The most traditional types of bread in Munich include large flour-dusted wheels of *Bauernbrot* ('farmer's bread'); the firm compact bodies of *Vollkorn* and *Sonnenblumenbrot* (wholewheat and sunflower-seed, respectively); *Pumpernickel*, a dark-brown rye with a slightly sweet

Dampfnudel, steamed dumplings served with custard

flavour; and *Brezeln*, pillowy pretzels sold warm out of the oven and studded with chunks of salt.

7. Bavarian desserts

Besides classic *Mehlspeisen* (baked treats) like the iconic strudel pastry, don't miss the *Dampfnudel*, a steamed dumpling served in a pool of custard sprinkled with cinnamon or poppyseeds. *Kaiserschmarrn* is another popular sweet option – shredded pancake sprinkled with raisins, dusted with sugar and drizzled with delicious plum compôte or apple sauce.

8. Breakfast

Frühstück, or breakfast, spans everything from mueslis, cereals and yoghurts to local bread served with jams, marmalade and honey, alongside cold cuts of ham and salami, liver sausage (*Leberwurst*), hard-boiled eggs, and *Weisswürste* (white sausage) with a dollop of sweet mustard. The most famous breakfast bread is *Pumpernickel* (dark-brown, slightly sweet rye loaf).

9. Soups

Bavarians know how to whip up hearty, tasty soups to nourish the soul in winter. Some of the top offerings are *Leberknödlsuppe*, a spicy liver dumpling soup; *Kartoffelsuppe*, a hearty mix of potatoes,

DINING ESSENTIALS

Many Germans like to eat their main meal in the middle of the day, and generally prefer a lighter supper (*Abendbrot*, or 'evening bread') of cold meats and cheeses, possibly eaten with a salad, in the evening. Restaurants in Munich are generally open for lunch and dinner without breaks, with some upmarket places only opening later in the evening. It's a good idea to reserve a table at smarter restaurants or in summer high season. Tipping is not expected, but adding ten to fifteen percent for good service will always be welcomed by the restaurant staff.

celery, leek and parsnip; and *Bohnensuppe*, made with white beans and sometimes pork rib or ham hock.

Smoked salmon on Pumpernickel

10. Beer

The highlight for many visitors to Munich is sampling the locally brewed Bavarian beers. Dunkles is dark beer with a slightly sweet, malty flavour; Helles is the more popular popular light lager; and Weissbier is a light, refreshing, slightly cloudy brew made from wheat and left to ferment in the bottle. Weissbier, mixed with lemonade, is known as a Russenmass, served by the litre. Helles and lemonade makes a shandy called Radler ('Cyclist').

To help you order

Waiter/waitress, please! **Bedienung, bitte.**
Could I/we have a table? **Ich hätte/Wir hätten gerne einen Tisch.**
The bill, please. **Zahlen, bitte.**
I would like … **Ich möchte gerne …**

beer **ein Bier**
bread **etwas Brot**
butter **etwas Butter**
cheese **Käse**
coffee **einen Kaffee**
cream **Sahne**
dessert **eine Nachspeise**
eggs **Eier**
fish **Fisch**
meat **Fleisch**
menu **die Karte**
milk **Milch**
mineral water **Mineralwasser**
mustard **etwas Senf**
pepper **Pfeffer**
potatoes **Kartoffeln**
salad **Salat**
salt **Salz**
soup **eine Suppe**
starter **eine Vorspeise**
tea **einen Tee**
wine **Wein**
vegetables **Gemüse**

... and read the menu

Apfel apple
Apfelsine orange
Aufschnitt cold cuts
Blaukraut red cabbage
Blumenkohl cauliflower
Braten roast (pork or beef)
Brat-kartoffeln roast potatoes
Ei/Eier egg/eggs
Geflügel poultry
Geräuchertes smoked meat
Gurkensalat cucumber salad
Hähnchen chicken (whole or half)
Kartoffel-knödel potato dumpling
Kraut cabbage
Lachs salmon
Lamm lamb
Rindfleisch beef
Rippchen smoked pork chops
Schinken ham
Schweine-fleisch pork
Semmel-knödel bread dumpling
Wild game
Wurst sausage

Places to eat

This selection features traditional Bavarian eateries, some of the major beer halls and beer gardens that are an important focal point of Munich life, as well as restaurants serving global cuisines. Each restaurant and café reviewed in this Guide is accompanied by a price category, based on the cost of a three-course meal (or similar) for two people, excluding drinks.

€€€€ = over €120
€€€ = €95–120
€€ = €70–95
€ = under €70

City centre

Alois Dallmayr Dienerstrasse 14–15, www.dallmayr.com. Restaurant above the sumptuous delicatessen of the same name, serving superb French cuisine. **€€€**

Altes Hackerhaus Sendlinger Strasse 14, www.hackerhaus.de. A venerable old tavern serving typical Bavarian cuisine, including calves' lung with bread dumplings and crispy roast pork knuckle. **€**

Augustiner Restaurant Neuhauser Strasse 27, www.augustiner-restaurant.com. This delightful old beer hall is a Munich favourite, serving Bavarian specialities in generous portions. Ask for a table in the little garden at the back by the fountain. **€€**

Bellevue di Monaco Müllerstrasse 2, www.bellevuedimonaco.de/cafe. Named after the views across the city from the rooftop terrace, this community centre has a ground-floor café run by refugees. It serves global food and drinks all day long, with vegetarian and vegan options. Saturday brunch is well worth a visit. **€€**

Brasserie Oskar Maria Salvatorplatz 1, www.oskarmaria.com. One of Munich's top gathering places, with the café dedicated to the writer Oskar Maria Graf (1894–1967). The restaurant offers a range of varied and imaginative dishes. **€€€**

Caspar Plautz Viktualienmarkt, stand 38, www.casparplautz.de. Lunchtime queues at this modest potato stall in Viktualienmarkt testify to the quality of its organic potato creations – arrive early to nab the potato of the day dish before it flies off the shelf. **€**

Conviva im Blauen Haus Hildegardstrasse 1, www.conviva-muenchen.de. Quality international dishes served in the Münchner Kammerspiele theatre restaurant, which employs and trains people with mental, psychological and other disabilities. The classic schnitzel is always on the menu. **€€**

Fraunhofer Fraunhoferstrasse 9, www.fraunhofertheater.de. A long-running institution with wood panelling, hunting trophies, chandeliers and huge windows. Great Bavarian food with many vegetarian options available. **€**

Galleria Sparkassenstrasse 11, www.ristorante-galleria.de. Upmarket Italian restaurant with excellent service and exciting, experimental cuisine. **€€€€**

Haxnbauer Tal 38, www.kuffler.de/de/haxnbauer. Old Bavarian tavern specialising in spit-roast meats and regional dishes. Reservations advisable. **€€**

Hofbräuhaus am Platzl Am Platzl 9, www.hofbraeuhaus.de. The mothership of all the world's beer halls, in traditional Bavarian oompah style, with live brass band music, waitresses dressed in traditional *Dirndl*, lashings of beer and local fare. An unmissable Munich experience. **€**

Komu Hackenstrasse 4, www.komu-restaurant.de. Tasting menus filled with surprising, inventive upmarket dishes, without wine pairing. On Saturday afternoon, come for the schnitzel with caviar and champagne. Reservations essential. **€€€€**

Mural Hotterstrasse 12, www.muralrestaurant.de. Upmarket seasonal cuisine made with fresh, organic ingredients sourced from small-scale suppliers and the nearby Viktualienmarkt. **€€€**

Nürnberger Bratwurst Glöckl am Dom Frauenplatz 9, www.bratwurst-gloeckl.de. Old tavern serving Bavarian specialities. Known particularly for its signature *Nürnberger Bratwurst* – and the Dürer prints on the wall. **€**

Pageou Kardinal-Faulhaber-Strasse 10, www.pageou.de. A well established, light and airy restaurant in the Fünf Höfe run by star chef Ali Güngörmüş. Creative interpretations of a range of cuisines. **€€€€**

Prince Myshkin Hackenstrasse 2, www.prinzmyshkin.com. Munich's best vegetarian haunt is a spacious and elegant affair, serving creative dishes ranging from Indian treats to a selection of *pinsa* pizzas to spinach and ricotta dumplings. Local and organic ingredients. **€**

Ratskeller Marienplatz 8, www.ratskeller.com. Underground labyrinthine restaurant tucked away in the cellar of the Neues Rathaus. You can eat in one of the large rooms with their vaulted ceilings, choose a more intimate booth or sit out in the pretty courtyard. Typically hearty Bavarian fare washed down with one-litre *Steins* of beer. **€€**

Spatenhaus an der Oper Residenzstrasse 12, www.kuffler.de/de/spatenhaus. A classic for a romantic dinner before or after visiting the opera opposite or one of the nearby theatres. Locals also love the cosy ground floor for morning snacks or lunches of expertly prepared Bavarian fare; upstairs is a more formal, elegant space for high-end dining. **€€€**

Weisses Bräuhaus Tal 7, www.schneider-brauhaus.de. Rambling old Bavarian-style beer hall serving its own Schneider Weissbier (wheat beer), including the ultra-strong and dark Aventinus. Great Bavarian and Austrian cuisine. **€**

Wirtshaus Maximilian Westermühlstraße 32, www.wirtshaus-maximilian.de. Convivial Bavarian haunt with excellent regional dishes, live music, and beer tapped from wooden kegs. **€€**

Zum Alten Markt Dreifaltigkeitsplatz 3, www.zumaltenmarkt.de. Popular restaurant decorated in hunting-lodge style, run by a young, female team. The grilled meats and salads are particularly good. **€€€**

Zum Spöckmeier Rosenstrasse 9, www.spoeckmeier.com. This atmospheric Bavarian place in the heart of Munich has been on the go since 1450. If you arrive before noon, try the home-made *Weisswurst*, but you can drop in any time of day or weekend night as food is served until the early hours. **€€**

The station and the southwest

Augustiner Bräustuben Landsberger Strasse 19, www.braeustuben.de. Possibly the city centre's most authentic beer hall adjoining the Augustiner brewery. Superb Bavarian food and understandably popular with locals and brewery workers. **€**

Chopan Elvirastrasse 18A, www.chopan.de. Munich has a large Afghan community whose restaurants provide a chance to sample the little-known cuisine of that country. A few streets northwest of the Hauptbahnhof, *Chopan* is the pick of the bunch, with tasty lamb and rice dishes. No alcohol. **€**

Hirschgarten Hirschgartenalle 1, https://hirschgarten.de. Munich's largest beer garden shaded by huge chestnut trees in the western district of

Laim, not far from Schloss Nymphenburg. There's seating for eight thousand and an adjoining game enclosure. **€**

La Favela Tumblingerstrasse 45, www.lafavela.de. Excellent authentic Brazilian cuisine served in an old U-Bahn train, surrounded by graffiti-covered containers in the quirky Bahnwärter Thiel district. **€€**

Löwenbräu-Keller Nymphenburger Strasse 2, www.loewenbraeukeller.com. Traditional Munich beer hall just west of the city centre, close to the Kunstareal museums. **€**

Schlosscafé im Palmenhaus Schlosspark Nymphenburg, www.palmenhaus.de. Romantic ambiance outside on the terrace as well as inside the big old glasshouse. **€€**

Taxisgarten Taxisstrasse 12, www.taxisgarten.de. Small but very popular beer garden in the western district of Neuhausen/Gern. **€**

Vinothek by Geisel Schützenstrasse 11, www.geisel-privathotels.de/vinothek. A classic Munich wine bar, just outside the main station, with seven hundred different German, French and Italian wines as well as great Italian and international meals. **€€€**

Isar and the east

Centro Espagñol Daiserstrasse 20, www.centroespanol.de. Small but long-established Spanish restaurant in the Sendling district, serving authentic Spanish cuisine. A variety of seafood, plus chicken and rabbit dishes and mouth-watering paella. **€€**

Hofbräukeller Innere Wiener Strasse 19, www.hofbraeukeller.de. Not to be confused with the Hofbräuhaus, this is a popular venue for beer-garden connoisseurs in the heart of Haidhausen. **€€**

Käfer-Schänke Prinzregentenstrasse 73, www.feinkost-kaefer.de/schaenke. Fine but casual dining in chalet-style surroundings on the upper floor of Gerd Käfer's gourmet department store near the Villa Stuck in Bogenhausen. Dishes inspired from around the world. **€€€€**

Klinglwirt Balanstrasse 16, www.klinglwirt.de. Bavarian and organic grub, with a strong focus on sustainable consumption, is what makes this informal Haidhausen eatery stand out from the crowd. Everything on the menu, from the schnitzel, fish and vegan dishes to the beer, is organic, regional and often seasonal. **€€**

Muffatwerk Zellstrasse 4, www.muffatwerk.de. Located near the Müller'sches Volksbad, this beer garden, café and cultural centre is the place to head for a night of alternative music, theatre and spoken word over a beer. **€**

Rue des Halles Steinstrasse 18, www.ruedeshalles.de. A bistro-type restaurant in Haidhausen serving good-quality French food, with traditional recipes rather than new culinary creations dominating the menu. **€€€€**

Zum Flaucher Isarauen 8, www.zumflaucher.de. South of the centre right next to the river, this is one of Munich's best beer gardens, popular among cyclists, walkers and bathers. Vegetarian and vegan options. **€**

Schwabing and the north

Bamberger Haus Brunnerstrasse 2, www.bambergerhaus.com. Restaurant with lovely *Biergarten* in an eighteenth-century Baroque villa in Luitpold Park (northwest of Schwabing). Bavarian and Alpine food, and excellent desserts. **€€€**

Chinesischer Turm Englischer Garten 3, www.chinaturm.de. One of Munich's first and largest beer gardens, in the heart of the Englischer Garten.

Guests can enjoy their drinks and typical Bavarian fare to a soundtrack of live music from the Bavarian band on the tower. Seven thousand seats. **€**

Halali Schönfeldstrasse 22, www.restaurant-halali.de. Traditional Munich restaurant in a baronial setting serving Bavarian dishes and inventive New German cuisine using local ingredients. Reservations recommended. **€€€**

Max-Emanuel Adalbertstrasse 33, www.max-emanuel.de. Pleasant and modern Bavarian restaurant and beer garden and tavern in the heart of Schwabing. **€€**

Portun Leopoldstrasse 150, www.portun-restaurant.de. Good-value fine-dining restaurant in Schwabing, serving dishes from the Alps, the Adriatic and the Balkans. **€€€**

Schwabinger Osterwaldgarten Keferstrasse 12, www.osterwaldgarten.de. A traditional restaurant and beer garden on the edge of the Englischer Garten, surrounded by ancient chestnut trees. Good food and excellent beer. **€€**

Tantris Johann-Fichte-Strasse 7, www.tantris.de. Superb Modern French cuisine prepared by one of Germany's top chefs and served in a contemporary restaurant with stark and startling decor. Outdoor dining. Reservations essential. **€€€€**

Zum Aumeister Sondermeierstrasse 9, www.aumeister.de. Favourite excursion destination on the northern edge of the English Garden, best reached by bike. The beer garden seats 2500. Cosy restaurant. **€**

Travel essentials

Practical information

Accessible travel

While most major museums, newer buildings and much of the public-transport system are wheelchair-friendly, the cobbled streets of the Old Town are difficult for wheelchair-users and those with mobility issues to navigate. Munich's Deutsche Bahn (DB) trains and stations are generally accessible to passengers with mobility impairments, including wheelchair-users. The company runs a 24-hour helpline (tel: 0180 6 51 25 12) or check the website (www.bahn.com), clicking on 'Services' and then 'Barrierefreies Reisen'; a multilingual app is also available for smartphones – search for "DB Barrierefrei". The website www.muenchen-barrierefrei.de has an overview of all accessible tourist offerings in Munich.

Accommodation

The Munich Tourist Office website (www.munich.travel) has extensive accommodation listings, with full details of amenities and prices. For the best rates online try www.booking.com. In addition to hotels, there are inns (*Gasthof*) and B&Bs (*Pension*). If you are touring Bavaria by car, look for '*Zimmer Frei*' (room to rent) signs. The Upper Bavaria Tourist Office lists places to stay at www.oberbayern.de.

I'd like a single/double room **Ich möchte bitte ein einzel-/ doppelzimmer.**
with bath/shower **mit bad/dusche**
What's the rate per night? **Wieviel kostet es pro nacht?**

Be aware that, in addition to the Oktoberfest, Munich hosts a variety of trade fairs and other events throughout the year, and so it's wise to check dates and book rooms as far in advance as possible.

Airport (see also Transport)

Munich Airport (MUC): www.munich-airport.de.
Getting into Munich. Munich Airport is 35km (22 miles) northeast of the

city centre. Suburban trains (S-Bahn) shuttle between the airport and the main railway station (Hauptbahnhof). The S-Bahn S8 runs every twenty minutes between the airport and Pasing via the centre; the S1 service approaches from the direction of Laim in the west, also three times an hour. Both stop at stations on the way. If you're getting off at Ostbahnhof or Marienplatz it's quicker to take the S8; for points west of Hauptbahnhof the S1 is the best option. Both services take about 45 minutes to reach Hauptbahnhof, and the journey costs €14.30 for a single ticket. A taxi takes around the same time but costs €60–70.

Apps

The official Munich city app (https://muenchen-app.swm.de) is handy for event listings and sight tickets. For navigating the public-transport network and purchasing tickets, the MVV-App (www.mvv-muenchen.de) is very handy; the excellent free Citymapper transport planning tool (www.citymapper.com) has live departure times. The official German taxi-hailing app (www.taxi.eu) is the surest way to secure a fairly priced ride; FREENOW (www.free-now.com) and Uber (www.uber.com) are both also available, but charge varying rates.

Where can I get a taxi? **Wo finde ich ein Taxi?**
How much is it to the centre? **Wieviel kostet es ins Zentrum?**

Bicycle hire

With some 1200km (800 miles) of bike paths and its relatively flat terrain, Munich is renowned for being a cyclists' city. Most roads have special cycle lanes, but as well as navigating town, a bike is great for exploring the banks of the River Isar and the Englischer Garten. The Tourist Information website (www.munich.travel) has suggested routes, bike rental and guided tours. Try Mike's Bike Tours (www.mikesbiketours.com) or Radius Bikes (www.radiustours.com). Nextbike (www.nextbike.de) has bikes for rent across the city.

Budgeting for your trip

Transport. MVV day tickets, valid on all forms of city transport, are a good deal if you are planning on making several journeys within 24 hours. The Airport-City-Day-Ticket (www.mvv-muenchen.de), which can be used across the entire network, costs €16.30, a regular day ticket for the city centre is €9.70.

Museums. Entry to most of Munich's attractions ranges from around €3 up to €18, with tickets for the main museums typically costing €10. Most of the museums located in the Kunstareal (and some outside) charge a symbolic €1 admission on Sundays. Ask about family tickets if travelling with children.

City cards. The Tourist Office's Munich Card and Munich City Pass offer free entry to, or discounts on, a variety of sights and tours, as well as optional public transport. The competing CityTourCard (www.citytourcard-muenchen.com) offers discounts of up to fifty percent on entry to sixty city attractions, as well as transport. It costs €18.50 a day or €30.50 for three days for the single adult inner-area version.

Accommodation. Double room per night: luxury €300–400, mid-range €140–250, budget €80–150, hostel bed €35.

Meals. For a three-course meal in a mid-range restaurant you can expect to pay around €45.

Drinks. Half-litre of beer €3.50–€5, coffee €2–3, bottle of wine from €14.

Car hire (see also Driving)

Unless you intend to visit extremely remote places in the Alps, Bavaria's public transport network makes renting a car a luxury you can afford to forego. If you do decide to rent a car, you'll need to have held a valid driver's licence for at least half a year; the minimum age is 19. Expect to pay from €35 per day for a medium-sized car if you haven't booked in advance online.

Renowned companies include Avis (www.avis.com), Enterprise (www.enterprise.de), Europcar (www.europcar.com), Hertz (www.hertz.de) and Sixt (www.sixt.com).

I'd like to rent a car **Ich möchte bitte ein Auto mieten.**
tomorrow **für morgen**
for one day/week **für einen Tag/für eine Woche**
Please include full insurance. **Bitte schliessen sie eine vollkaskoversicherung ab.**

Climate

Munich's climate can swing from one extreme to another, from the bitterest cold in winter to hot and dry or muggy in summer. The dry, warm wind from the south, known as *Föhn*, can result in very pleasant conditions wonderful for visitors.

Munich's average temperatures are given below.

	J	F	M	A	M	J	J	A	S	O	N	D
°C	1	3	9	14	18	21	23	23	20	13	7	2
°F	34	37	48	57	64	70	73	73	68	55	45	35

Crime and safety

Compared to many urban centres, Munich's crime rate is quite low. Nonetheless, it's advisable to take all the normal precautions. Don't leave money or valuables in your car or hotel room; lock them in the safe instead. If you are robbed, report the incident to staff at the hotel reception and the nearest police station. The police will provide you with a certificate to present to your insurance company, or to your consulate if your passport has been stolen.

I want to report a theft. **Ich möchte einen Diebstahl melden.**
My handbag/wallet/passport has been stolen.
Meine Handtasche/Brieftasche/mein Pass ist gestohlen worden

Driving

To bring your car into Germany you will need a national driver's licence (or international for those coming from the US, Australia, South Africa or other foreign countries); vehicle registration papers; a national identity car sticker; a red warning triangle in case of breakdown; and a first-aid kit.

Insurance. Third-party insurance is compulsory.

Low emission sticker. Driving inside Munich's Mittlere Ring (ring road) requires a low-emission sticker to be displayed prominently on the windscreen (available online at www.umwelt-plakette.de).

Driving regulations. Drive on the right, pass on the left. When driving on the Autobahn (motorway, expressway), passing another vehicle on the right is strictly prohibited. In the absence of traffic lights, or stop or give-way signs, vehicles coming from the right have priority at intersections, unless otherwise indicated. At roundabouts (traffic circles), approaching cars must always give way to traffic that is already in the circle, unless otherwise stated. Trams must be passed on the right and never at a stop (unless there's a traffic island).

Driving licence **Führerschein**
Car registration papers **Kraftfahrzeugpapiere**

Speed limits. The speed limit is 100km/h (62mph) on all open roads except for motorways and divided highways, where there's no limit unless otherwise indicated (the suggested maximum speed is 130km/h, or 81mph). In town, the limit is 50km/h (31mph), except on the Mittlerer Ring, the six-lane ring road system around the city, where the limit is 60km/h (37mph).

Einbahnstrasse One-way street
Einordnen Get into lane
Fussgänger Pedestrians
Kurzparkzone Short-term parking
Links fahren Keep left

Parken verboten No parking
Umleitung Detour
Vorsicht Caution

Breakdowns. In the event of a breakdown on the Autobahn and other important roads, use one of the emergency telephones located every second kilometre (the direction of the nearest one is indicated by a small arrow on the reflector poles at the roadside).

Ask for Strassenwacht, run jointly by the two German automobile clubs ADAC and AVD. Assistance is free; towing and spare parts have to be paid for. For round-the-clock breakdown service, visit www.adac.de or call tel: +49 89 22 22 22.

Where's the nearest car park? **Wo ist der nächste Parkplatz/ Parkhaus?**
Full tank, please. **Bitte volltanken.**
Super/lead-free/diesel **Super/bleifreies Benzin/Diesel**
I've had a breakdown. **Ich habe eine Pane.**
There's been an accident. **Es ist ein Unfall passiert.**

Electricity

Germany has 220-volt, 50-cycle AC. Plugs are the standard continental Europe type for which both British and North American appliances need an adaptor.

Embassies and consulates

Canada: Tal 29, tel: (089) 219 9570.
Ireland: Brienner St 45 A–D, tel: (089) 2080 5990.
South Africa: Sendlinger-Tor-Platz 5, tel: (089) 231 1630.
UK: Möhlstrasse 5, tel: (089) 211090.
US: Königinstrasse 5, tel: (089) 28880.

Emergencies

Emergency telephone numbers:

Police: 112 or 110; Fire and emergency medical services: 112

I need a doctor **Ich brauche einen Arzt**
an ambulance **einen Krankenwagen**
a hospital **ein Krankenhaus**

Getting there

By air. Munich Airport is a major hub, receiving many European and intercontinental flights a day. However, the main airport for transatlantic flights is still Frankfurt, from where several flights a day connect to Munich. Average travel time from London to Munich is 1hr 30min, from New York 9hr. British Airways (www.britishairways.com), easyJet (www.easyjet.com), Monarch (www.monarch.co.uk) and Lufthansa (www.lufthansa.com) all link Munich with London (all airports except City), Birmingham, Leeds/Bradford, Edinburgh and Manchester.

By coach. Bavarian company FlixBus (www.flixbus.de) runs regular coaches from London via Frankfurt or Paris to Munich. The trip takes approximately 24hr.

By rail. It's easy to travel from London to Munich by train in a day. Eurostar links London with Brussels in just 2hr 30min, then high-speed ICE trains link Brussels to Munich via Cologne or Frankfurt in just six hours more. Or you can travel overnight from London to Munich with just one change – simply take a late-afternoon Eurostar from the English capital to Paris or Brussels then an overnight sleeping-car or couchette on to Munich. Reservations are obligatory on all Eurostar and night services' check the Seat 61 website (www.seat61.com) for more information.

Guides and tours

Hop-on, hop-off bus tours run by Gray Line (www.stadtrundfahrten-muenchen.de) and CitySightseeingMunich (www.citysightseeing-munich-com) depart from outside the main railway station. There are various itineraries available, taking in the city centre sights as well as peripheral attractions such as the Olympiapark, Schloss Nymphenburg and the Bavaria Filmstadt.

Cycling and walking tours are also available, several free of charge. Mike's Bike Tours (www.mikesbiketours.com) and Radius Tours (www.radiustours.com) all offer classic and themed routes.

Health and medical care

Germany has free reciprocal health agreements with other EU member states, whose citizens can apply for a free European Health Insurance Card (EHIC) in advance of a trip. UK citizens need a GHIC (Global Health Insurance Card), which is available free via the NHS website and offers access to accident and emergency care along with certain routine healthcare. Even if you have EU healthcare privileges in Germany, an insurance policy is a wise precaution to cover against theft, loss and illness or injury.

Pharmacies are open during normal shopping hours. At night, on Sundays and on public holidays, all pharmacies display the address of the nearest one that is open. Pharmacies located close to the main train station include: Inter Apotheke, Elisenstrasse 5, www.inter-apotheke.de; and Schützen Apotheke, Schützenstrasse 5, www.schuetzenapotheke-muenchen.de.

Bavarian tap water is perfectly safe to drink; only rarely will you see the sign 'Kein Trinkwasser' (which means 'not drinking water', usually at public squares and on trains).

Where's the nearest (all-night) pharmacy? **Wo ist die nächste Apotheke (mit Nachtdienst)?**

Language

About one-third of the Munich population speaks a form of Bavarian dialect. Real Bavarian is difficult to understand, even for the many Northern Germans who live in Munich, but Bavarians can often be persuaded to speak something closer to standard German. English is widely understood and spoken, and most of the larger shops, hotels and restaurants have English-speaking staff, but don't take it for granted. Showing a willingness to use simple Bavarian or German phrases will go a long way.

LGBTQ+ travellers

Munich has an open atmosphere and is very accepting of all. In particular, the Glockenbachviertel district around Gärtnerplatz has many LGBTQ+ restaurants and clubs. The official Tourist Office website (www.munich.travel) has tips for LGBTQ+ visitors.

Do you speak English? **Sprechen sie Englisch?**

Money

Currency. Germany's monetary unit is the euro (€), which is divided into 100 cents. Coins: 1, 2, 5, 10, 20 and 50 cents, and €1 and 2. Notes: €5, 10, 20, 50, 100, 200 and 500.

Can I pay with this credit card? **Kann ich mit dieser Kreditkarte bezahlen?**
I want to change some pounds/dollars. **Ich möchte Pfund/ Dollar wechseln.**
Where's the nearest bank/currency exchange office? **Wo ist die nächste Bank/Wechselstube?**
Is there a cash machine near here? **Gibt es hier einen Geldautomaten?**
How much is that? **Wieviel kostet das?**

Banks and currency exchange. Foreign currency can be changed at banks *(Bank)*, savings banks *(Sparkasse)*, currency exchange offices *(Wechselstube)* and at some hotels and post offices, but check rates and commission fees carefully. Using a fee-free card from a bank like Wise or Revolut is a better option. Take your passport with you to change money.

Opening times

Museum hours vary, but are usually from 9.30am–5pm or 6pm. Most have one late-closing day and are shut on Mondays. **Shops** are generally open from 9 or 10am–8pm, Monday to Friday, and till 4pm (some till 12.30pm) on Saturdays. Shops that are outside the main shopping areas in Munich usually close between 1 and 3pm.

Police

The police emergency number is **110**; Munich's central police station (*Polizeipräsidium*) is located at Ettstrasse 2, close to the Frauenkirche.

> Where's the nearest police station? **Wo ist die nächste Polizeistation?**

Public holidays

1 January **Neujahr** New Year's Day
6 January **Heilige Drei Könige** Epiphany
1 May **Tag der Arbeit** Labour Day
15 August **Mariä Himmelfahrt** Assumption Day
3 October **Nationalfeiertag** Reunification Day
1 November **Allerheiligen** All Saints' Day
25, 26 December **Weihnachten** Christmas

Movable dates

Karfreitag Good Friday
Ostermontag Easter Monday
Christi Himmelfahrt Ascension Day
Pfingstmontag Whit Monday
Fronleichnam Corpus Christi

Telephone

The dialling code for Germany is 49. The dialling code for Munich from outside the city is 089. For international calls from Munich, dial 00 before the country code (44 for UK, 1 for US), then the area code and number of your destination. Roaming charges may apply for calls and data in the EU. Purchasing an e-SIM or a local SIM card can save you money if you plan to use lots of data or make many calls.

Time zones

Germany follows Central European Time (GMT + 1). In summer, the clock is put one hour ahead (GMT + 2):

New York	London	**Munich**	Jo'burg	Sydney	Auckland
6am	11am	**noon**	noon	8pm	10pm

Tipping

While waiters, porters and other service providers don't expect tips, it is always warmly appreciated. Service is normally included in the price at restaurants; check the bill.

Toilets

Toilets may be labelled with symbols of a man or a woman or the initials WC. Otherwise, *Herren* (gentlemen) and *Damen* (ladies) or a double zero (00) sign are indicated.

Where are the toilets? **Wo sind die Toiletten?**

Tourist information

The Munich Tourist Board (www.muenchen.de) maintains two information offices in the city, located at Hauptbahnhof railway station, Bahnhofsplatz 2 and in the Town Hall, Marienplatz 2.

For information about Southern Bavaria, visit the Munich–Upper Bavaria Tourist Association website www.oberbayern.de.

The German National Tourist Board (www.germany.travel) maintains offices in many countries; check your nearest online.

Transport

Munich is served by a highly efficient network of buses, trams, U-Bahn (underground railway) and S-Bahn (suburban railway, all coordinated by the MVV (Munich Transport and Tariff Association, www.mvv-muenchen.de). The U- and S-Bahn serve the city centre, while the S-Bahn connects to the suburbs and surrounding countryside.

All forms of public transport operate from about 5am to 1am daily, with special night services till around 4am. Free maps and travel information are available at the tourist offices. Your ticket is not checked as you board, but random checks are carried out. Fines are automatic if you are not able to produce a valid ticket when asked.

What's the fare to ... ? **Wieviel kostet es nach ...?**
Where is the nearest bus stop? **Wo ist die nächste Bushaltestelle?**
When's the next bus to ...? **Wann geht der nächste Bus nach...?**
I want a ticket to ... **Ich will eine Fahrkarte nach ...**
single/return **einfache Karte/Rückfahrkarte**
Will you tell me when to get off? **Könnten Sie mir bitte sagen, wann ich aussteigen muss.**

Tickets, interchangeable between U-Bahn, S-Bahn, buses and trams, entitle users to free transfers for up to three hours in one zone, four hours in two and more zones, so long as you travel in the same direction. It's easiest to buy tickets from the MVV-App or alternatively from the big blue vending machines at U- and S-Bahn stations or on buses and at tram stops, hotels, tobacconists, newsagents and stationers that display a white 'K'. Vending machines are marked *Einzelfahrkarte* (single ticket) or *Streifenkarte* (strip ticket). The latter works out cheaper if you intend to make several trips, or when you travel as a group.

Be sure to cancel paper tickets in the blue cancelling machines positioned at platform entrances and in buses and trams; if you have a strip ticket you need to cancel two strips per zone travelled (persons aged 15 to 20 years cancel only one strip per zone, children one strip per trip), unless you travel only one stop by U- or S-Bahn or two stops by bus or tram – then one strip is sufficient.

Visas and entry requirements

Germany is part of the Schengen area, meaning there are no limitations on the amount of time EU citizens can spend there. Travellers from the UK, US, Canada, Australia, New Zealand can stay visa-free for up to ninety days within any 180-day period. South Africans need to apply for a Schengen visa.

By the end of 2026, all non-EU citizens travelling under the 90/180-day rule will need to apply for a €7 ETIAS prior to arrival. Similar to the ESTA system in the US, this travel authorisation requires an online registration and payment before you travel, and it is valid for three years. A new ETIAS is required if you change your passport.

Index

MINI
MUNICH & BAVARIA

First Edition 2025

Editor: Joanna Reeves
Author: Jack Altman
Updater: Jeroen van Marle
Picture Editor: Piotr Kala
Picture Manager: Tom Smyth
Cartography Update: Katie Bennett
Layout: Danielle Titmas
Production Operations Manager: Katie Bennett
Publishing Technology Manager: Rebeka Davies
Head of Publishing: Sarah Clark
Photography Credits: Apa 48, 54, 56, 61, 78, 113; Deutsches Museum 75; Dreamstime 90, 94, 98; iStock 7, 12CL, 12TR, 12BR, 13T, 13B, 14T, 14BR 14BL, 41, 68, 80, 85, 88, 104; Public domain 13CT, 28, 30, 65; Ra Boe/Wikipedia 21; Shutterstock 1, 9, 11, 12TL, 12CR, 12BL, 13CB, 14CL, 16T, 16CL, 16BR, 16BL, 18T, 18CL, 18BR 18BL, 23, 24, 25, 27, 33, 35, 37, 38, 42, 44, 45, 49, 51, 52, 59, 62, 64, 66, 71, 72, 76, 79, 82, 86, 87, 95, 96, 99, 100, 101, 102, 106, 108, 110, 114, 115, 116, 117, 118, 119, APA/Glyn Genin 46, 92, 97
Cover Credits: The Frauenkirche **Shutterstock**

About the author

Travel writer, editor and tour guide Jeroen van Marle grew up in England, studied geography in the Netherlands and hitchhiked everywhere between Sofia and St Petersburg before settling in Berlin, after moving 28 times between eight countries and across three continents. He started his writing career with the InYourPocket.com city guide to Bucharest in the 1990s and has worked on multiple Rough Guides titles since.

Distribution

UK, Ireland and Europe: Apa Publications (UK) Ltd; mail@roughguides.com
United States and Canada: Two Rivers; ips@ingramcontent.com
Australia and New Zealand: Woodslane; info@woodslane.com.au
Worldwide: Apa Publications (UK) Ltd; mail@roughguides.com

EU Representative

LOGOS EUROPE, 9 rue Nicolas Poussin, 17000, LA ROCHELLE, France; Contact@logoseurope.eu; +33 (0) 667937378

Special Sales, Content Licensing and CoPublishing

Rough Guides can be purchased in bulk quantities at discounted prices. We can create special editions, personalized jackets and corporate imprints tailored to your needs.
mail@roughguides.com
roughguides.com

Printed by Finidr in Czech Republic

ISBN: 9781835292501

This book was produced using **Typefi** automated publishing software.

A catalogue record for this book is available from the British Library

Contact us

Every effort has been made to ensure that this publication is accurate, free from safety risks, and provides accurate information. However, changes and errors are inevitable. The publisher is not responsible for any resulting loss, inconvenience, injury or safety concerns arising from the use of this book. If you notice any errors, outdated information, or potential safety risks, please send your comments with the subject line "Rough Guide Mini Munich & Bavaria Update" to mail@roughguides.com.